A SEASON IN THE BIG HOUSE

An Unscripted Insider Look
at the
Marvel of Michigan Football

George Cantor

TRIUMPH
B O O K S
CHICAGO

Library of Congress Cataloging-in-Publication Data

Cantor, George, 1941–
    A season in the big house : an unscripted insider look at the
marvel of Michigan football / George Cantor.
        p. cm.
    ISBN-13: 978-1-57243-840-8 (hard cover)
    ISBN-10: 1-57243-840-1 (hard cover)
    1. University of Michigan—Football—History. 2. Michigan
Wolverines (Football team)—History. I. Title.
    GV958.U52863C367 2006
    796.332′630977435—dc22

                                                    2006005609

This book is available in quantity at special discounts for your
group or organization. For further information, contact:

Triumph Books
542 South Dearborn Street
Suite 750
Chicago, Illinois 60605
(312) 939-3330
Fax (312) 663-3557

Printed in U.S.A.
ISBN-13: 978-1-57243-840-8
ISBN-10: 1-57243-840-1
Design by Sue Knopf
Photos courtesy of AP/Wide World Photos unless otherwise
indicated. Chapter opener stadium photo courtesy of the
University of Michigan/Bentley Library Archives.

*For Caryn Rachel,
the newest Wolverine*

Contents

Introduction vii

Chapter 1
This One's for All 111,000 of You 1

Chapter 2:
September 3: Michigan 33, Northern Illinois 17 23

Chapter 3
September 10: Notre Dame 17, Michigan 10 45

Chapter 4
September 17: Michigan 55, Eastern Michigan 0. 57

Chapter 5
October 1: Michigan 34, Michigan State 31 75

Chapter 6
October 8: Minnesota 23, Michigan 20 89

Chapter 7
October 15: Michigan 27, Penn State 25 105

Chapter 8
October 22: Michigan 23, Iowa 20 121

Chapter 9
October 29: Michigan 33, Northwestern 17 131

Chapter 10
November 12: Michigan 41, Indiana 14 147

Chapter 11
November 19: Ohio State 25, Michigan 21 169

Chapter 12
December 28: Alamo Bowl, Nebraska 32, Michigan 28 . . . 177

Afterword 181

Lloyd Carr Reflects. 187

Appendix: 2005 Statistics 197

Introduction

The most shocking moment I experienced in writing this book came when someone compared the University of Michigan football program to the New York Yankees.

This staggered me. Not only staggered, but sickened.

I was a well-brought-up child of Detroit, taught by my father that the Yankees were to be regarded as objects of hatred. They were arrogant and soulless in their perfection. They blighted every summer of my life from the time I became aware of baseball until I graduated from college. In those 16 years they won the pennant every season but two. My Tigers bobbed up and down between second-rate play and occasional contention. On those rare instances that they seemed about to challenge the Yanks, they were swatted away like the pesky insects they were.

A college friend said that rooting for the Yankees was like rooting for General Motors. (Of course, given the recent history of GM, that comparison isn't especially apt anymore.)

The lesson learned from those years, however, was that precious moments of intense joy are paid for many times over by years of anguish.

Anguish is not generally a word used in the same sentence as *Yankees fan.* But you do become closely acquainted with it in Ann Arbor.

I know this because I was also taught by my father to cheer for the Wolverines. I could never quite figure out why he was so attached to them. He didn't go to Michigan, and neither did I. We were both graduates of Wayne State University and proud fans of the Tartars.

Well, at least we used to be. The school grew weary of having its nickname confused with the gunk on your teeth and the stuff you put on fish, so several years ago it changed its name to Warriors. So I am now a proud Warrior—yes!

Still, Wayne is a commuter campus, and although it is a major university with excellent professional schools and research facilities, it plays Division II football. I have attended exactly two Wayne State football games in my life. One was to meet a girl in 1960, and the other was to cover a contest at Eastern Illinois in 1967. They lost both times, and the girl wasn't that great, either.

Faced with this vast emptiness in my collegiate loyalties, I followed Dad's example and turned to Michigan. I was nine years old at the time, and that Michigan team happened to go to the Rose Bowl and beat California.

This indicated to me that I had chosen wisely. Not that I was all that wrapped up in it. Neither the infamous Snow Bowl game of that 1950 season at Ohio State nor the ensuing Rose Bowl was televised. Still, I do have a vague recollection of listening to the game in Pasadena on the radio and being immensely cheered at the outcome.

I could not have known it, but Michigan was about to enter the longest fallow period in its history. It would be another 14 years before it returned to the Rose Bowl, and losing seasons would become commonplace.

Michigan State, at the exact same time, was turning into a national power. Two years after I chose Michigan as the team of my heart, the Spartans won the national championship. In the very next season, their first in the Big Ten, they won the conference title and went to the Rose Bowl.

Many of my peers quickly became big Michigan State fans. But I had made my choice, and even at that tender age it seemed shallow to cast it aside so quickly. I felt I was a better person than that. The born-again MSU converts were like the kids who showed up at our softball games wearing Yankees caps. They never actually got beaten up, but they were despised as front-running geeks.

Still, it was hard. In 1955, for example, Michigan won its first six games and was ranked number one in the country. It was a magnificent crew, led by All-American ends Ron Kramer and Tom Maentz. Their pictures appeared on the cover of *Sports Illustrated*. I went to my first game in The Big House that fall and watched them dismantle Army, 26–2.

Then they went down to Champaign and were simply corked by a nondescript Illinois team, 25–6. I was keeping score of this mess at home, and at one point in the fourth quarter simply hurled my notebook across the room in a rage and switched off the radio. It was a course of action I would come to repeat all too often.

Incidentally, Em Lindbeck, the Illinois quarterback who directed this disaster, became a baseball player. His only two games in the majors were with the Tigers. He batted once and failed to get a hit. It figures.

Michigan also lost its final game that year to Ohio State. This was during the very core of the era in which Woody Hayes had decided the forward pass was an unmanly fad that was not properly part of football. He simply rammed the ball down Michigan's throat and dared them to stop him. They could not.

This is also the year I learned not to like Ohio State very much. If any fair correlation to the Yankees can be drawn, it is with that school. George Steinbrenner is a graduate of Ohio State and an avid Buckeyes fan. Michigan supporters are absolutely convinced that he signed Drew Henson to a whopping baseball contract for the sole purpose of leaving the team without an experienced quarterback.

There is, however, a slight basis for the comparison to the Yankees. They had a losing season in 1925, when Babe Ruth went down with a "bellyache" that was later revealed to be venereal disease. They didn't have another one until 1965—39 years in a row without a losing record. The Wolverines last had a losing season in 1967. Going into 2006, that makes 38 years in a row.

Very impressive. But now we get to the anguish part.

While the Yankees won 19 championships during their streak, Michigan has won only one. In their final game of the season during that time, either against OSU or in a bowl game, their mark is 14–23–1.

So you see, those who speak of the Yankees are simply clueless. It's more like being an Atlanta Braves fan. You win every year except when it comes to the games that matter.

Bo Schembechler pointed out, however, that not one of those end-of-the-season losses cost Michigan a national championship. Even though he went into the last game with a perfect record five straight times between 1970 and 1974, and then lost or tied it, the title would have gone elsewhere even if Michigan had won. Never were they ranked higher than third before any of these sad finales. In fact, the latest that a Schembechler team held the number-one spot was November 6, 1977, when they lost at Purdue, 16–14, on a missed field goal at the gun.

I can still hear Bob Ufer's mournful cry into the mike. "No good," he muttered. "No good. No good."

Since Schembechler's retirement, even accounting for the 1997 championship year, Michigan has been ranked first for a grand total of only four weeks.

It isn't as if they always fall short. It's more a case of—you know—things happening. Bad things.

So while some may call Michigan fans arrogant asses, we know in our hearts, as George Will once wrote about following the Chicago Cubs, that man is not born to pleasure.

My intention in writing this book was to get at the mystique of being a Michigan fan. There are so damn many of us, and we are so disposed to hope for the best and expect the worst.

Predictions for the 2005 season were typically bubbly, and it appeared that it could be a year worth remembering.

That prediction turned out to be correct, but for all the wrong reasons. No one anticipated a season that resembled a tightrope walker with the DTs. At times it seemed it would all plunge to ruin, and at others it appeared that the safety of the far side was only a shaky step away.

Neither turned out to be true. Absolutely stirring victories were outweighed by absolutely crushing losses. It sometimes seemed as if we were witnessing the end of an era of Michigan dominance and the start of a slow descent into the ordinary. Either that or it was the most god-awful streak of bad luck ever to hit a football team.

Maybe both. It was hard to tell.

Ambiguity has entered the equation, and it will take another season or two to learn whether it has taken up permanent residence in Ann Arbor.

This One's for
All 111,000 of You

very season begins like a bright promise, clean as a freshly laundered uniform, free of the grime of failure. It's true in any sport, even in places where teams have been beaten down for decades, deprived of the slightest whiff of success.

Whether it's the Chicago Cubs or the Arizona Cardinals or the Temple Owls, at the beginning, their fans can hope, if only blindly and for a little while. Before the first ball is snapped or the first pitch is thrown, it is still a world of limitless possibilities. Maybe this will be the year when reality gets stood on its head, the losers rise up, and the last shall be first.

1

When August winds down in Ann Arbor, however, there is a different sort of anticipation. No less keen, but pitched to another key.

Success is regarded as merely the starting point for University of Michigan football. That is the given. The only question is a matter of degree.

What will it be? A share of the Big Ten title? Another trip to Pasadena? A shot at number one?

What will it be? 10–2? 11–1? 12–0?

Because 9–3 is not so good, and 8–4 is abject failure, unacceptable. Something less than that—be serious. It can't happen.

A record that would send fans into gleeful dances and a December bowl game at other places is met here with scowls of contempt. The destination is always January. That certainty not only brings in the prime-time recruits, it fills more stadium seats than any other team in college football. Everybody wants to be a part of the spectacle at The Big House.

They troop in, 111,000 strong, every autumn Saturday when the gates open, because they know this is a place where failure isn't allowed. Nowhere else are expectations constantly pegged so high.

Once upon a time it used to be that way at Notre Dame, and maybe, to some extent, with the Yankees. But even the Yankees can falter. The Wolverines never do.

Michigan has been to a bowl game every season since 1975—which was the first year the Big Ten lifted its restriction on postseason participation. They haven't missed once, and 13 times in those 30 seasons it was the Rose Bowl.

Their last losing season was 1967. That was two years BB—Before Bo. That's the longest such streak in any sport.

Even in the worst year, the injury-plagued, 6–6 1984 season, Brigham Young had to beat Michigan in the Holiday Bowl before it could claim the national title.

Nebraska fell from this list in 2004. It was the first time the Huskers had lost more than they won since 1961—four national championships ago. In Lincoln, some would say five and tick off the 1997 season, too, when they finished first in the coaches' poll. This is a point that does not even merit discussion in Ann Arbor, which was number one in the AP balloting that year. There was barely disguised glee at Michigan when Nebraska toppled, because some felt it was payback for such hubris, coming seven years overdue.

What rankles, however, is that through all those seasons of success there has been only one national title. That is the other part of the equation. It's always something, some unexpected calamity that shatters hopes and turns championship aspirations into mere excellence once again. It shapes autumn in Ann Arbor—a worm-infested apple that falls to the ground and sours the entire season.

On the other hand, it keeps 'em coming back. Baseball executives like to say the perfect season is one in which your team is in the pennant race all the way but finishes second. That type of finish fills the stadium, and no one gets jaded, which pretty much fits the annual scenario at Michigan.

"You are part of the largest crowd to watch a football game anywhere in the United States today," the public-address announcer always reminds the throng as he announces the official attendance total in the fourth quarter.

The last game played before anything less than a six-figure sellout in Ann Arbor took place on October 25, 1975. A

3

paltry 93,857 showed up to watch the ritual dismemberment of always sad Indiana, 55–7.

Michael Ben has the date committed to memory. He was born exactly two weeks later, on the very day Michigan began its 30-year streak of six-figure sellouts. "When Michael was four years old, his nursery-school teacher asked him to draw a picture of a family activity," says his mother, Barbara. "He turned in a picture of all of us at Michigan Stadium, waving our arms and cheering.

"The thing was, he had never even been to a Michigan game yet. When the teacher showed us the drawing, we figured we'd better take him."

In his freshman year at Michigan, Mike showed up for the home opener with a maize-and-blue block M painted on his chest in zinc oxide. ("All the stores seemed to be out of paint.") It was September 4, a hot late-summer afternoon. As he glumly watched Michigan lose to Notre Dame, the sun beat down on the student section. At day's end he found that it had baked the pigment into his skin.

"For the rest of the year, I was known in the dorm as Michigan Mike, the guy with the M on his chest," he says. "I thought of it as a mark of dedication. I don't know how other people thought of it."

He and his brother, Josh, have a little ritual. When either of them makes his first visit to The Big House each season, he calls the other's cell phone and says: "This is the greatest sight these eyes have ever seen."

It's a line from the movie *Rudy*. Of course, *Rudy* was about Notre Dame football. No matter. The sentiment is the same.

A little more than two months before the 2005 opening game, Michael moved back to Michigan after eight years of exile at law school and work on the East Coast. He does not paint his chest anymore. But under the skin his heart is pumping maize and blue.

And the rate speeds up in late August.

Fan Day 2005: August 27

It was a rainy Saturday morning. We debated whether it was even worth making the drive to Ann Arbor to attend. Who would be crazy enough to show up on a crummy day like that?

Usually this is an important day for the big spenders in the Victors Club. These are the fans who support Michigan football to the tune of a $15,000 donation. (For a mere $85,000 more one can join the Champions Club and go directly to heaven.) In return the Victors get the right to buy season tickets between the 30-yard lines, prime parking spots, and first crack at tickets to big road games and the inevitable bowl. There is also a meeting with the coaching staff, which gives them an insider's view of the season to come. Lunch is served, and everyone goes away jolly.

Other fans of lesser means, many of whom are overjoyed to score a ticket for any game on any yard line, normally get to enter The Big House for autographs on Media Day after the press concludes its work. But because of construction of a new reception center for recruits, university officials decided this year that they could not safely handle all of this vast horde on the same day.

So the Victors Club event and Media Day were rescheduled. For the first time the average fans were given a day all their own, on the Saturday before the opener.

They would enter the stadium through the players' tunnel, and even get to walk upon the hallowed turf, composed now of recycled material from old tires. The gates would open at 10:30 AM, and they would have 90 minutes to take care of business. The scoreboard clocks would count the time down, just as they do in the long minutes before kickoff on game days.

At the very worst, we figured, if no one else chose to show up in the persistent drizzle, we would drive over to Angelo's, the celebrated campus hangout, and observe the morning with an order of raisin French toast.

We found a parking place easily enough and had to walk just one block to the stadium. It appeared that we were right on time and ready to walk right in. That's when security told us to get right to the end of the line.

"Some of these folks have been waiting for hours," said the guard, who seemed somewhat overwhelmed. An easy morning duty stationed outside the stadium had turned into an unanticipated exercise in massive crowd control.

The line wound all the way through the Champions' and Victors' parking lots, down a walkway, and beyond the farthest end of Crisler Arena. Most of it was composed of people in Michigan colors. A good many of them were accompanied by similarly clad toddlers. Significant numbers of the latter group were not yet ambulatory and were being conveyed into the stadium in baby strollers.

It seemed that no one had expected this sort of turnout— not on the first time it had been tried, on a muggy morning, with heavier rain in the forecast.

As the line shuffled along the walkway to Schembechler Hall, the base of football operations, the team strode past dressed in game jerseys and shorts. They seemed bemused by this mob of civilians who had turned out for no other reason than to get a good look at them and to have them sign a ball, a photograph, a shirt—anything they could get their hands on that spoke of Michigan football.

Steve Clark and his two-year-old son were both dressed in full Wolverines gear. Once inside Clark planned to have the tyke line up opposite him on the goal line in a three-point stance while his wife, Kristina, snapped a picture.

"I didn't go to school here," he said. "But I grew up in Ann Arbor. My earliest memories are of game days, and how excited both my parents were, and the whole neighborhood dressed up in maize and blue. And I remember the disbelief and sorrow from my dad every time they lost.

"We planned our wedding around the football schedule. It had to be on a weekend that they were playing a road game."

Although he went to Ball State University (because "priorities change and it has a great communications program"), Clark came home to host a pregame show on a local radio station for several years. He has been a season-ticket holder since 1985.

So did he pick out an appropriate Wolverines name for his first-born son? Desmond? Braylon? Lloyd?

Clark looked sheepish.

"Ahhh, we decided to call him Hayden," he said, with a nod toward his wife. Among this mighty throng of Michigan faithful, she was wearing an Iowa T-shirt.

"But she swore to me it was an old family name," Clark added quickly. "It has absolutely nothing to do with Hayden Fry."

7

Kristina smiled—a small, secret Hawkeyes smile.

As the crowd continued inching forward, people got out their cell phones to describe the scene to the folks back home.

"There have got to be 100,000 people lined up here," said the guy behind us in line. "No, make that 200,000. I've never seen anything like this, man."

The estimate that appeared on Michigan websites the next day placed the crowd at closer to 10,000. But Michigan fans are used to expansive figures.

As we approached the tunnel the phones fell silent, and it wasn't only because they wouldn't work in there. No, it was something more than that. It was because of where we were walking.

This is where the players come rushing out on Saturdays, shouldering their way through the narrow locker room door ("No admittance except Michigan football personnel"), and then running side by side through the tunnel before finally bursting, like huge corks released from a pressurized bottle, onto the turf.

The roar of 111,000 builds and "The Victors" blares and coaches and players alike leap to touch the M Club banner under which they all must pass to reach the far sideline. It is one of the great moments in college football.

The stands were empty as we entered. The band wasn't playing, although the cheerleading squad was on the field going through some routines. But as we emerged under the gray morning sky again, there was just the smallest taste of what it must feel like to make that entrance and realize you have entered The Big House before "the largest crowd to watch a football game anywhere in the United States today." The aura lingers, even now.

Lloyd Carr was seated just to the left of the tunnel exit. The autograph line in front of him already extended all the way across the field. He was signing with a look of grim determination on his face; another hour and a half to get through, this irreplaceable time subtracted from the urgent business at hand—preparing for the opener, getting ready for Notre Dame, going over reports on recruits, talking to his staff. He was trying to be congenial, but still, he bore the look of a man who could hardly wait to get out of there. That look comes with the territory when you are the football coach at Michigan.

Another long line seemed to snake randomly across the turf with no apparent destination. Who was waiting on the far end?

"Mike Hart," said one of the standees. "At least, I hope so."

There really was no way of telling. Not until you got there. You took your place in line as an act of faith. Surely, it would lead to someone. All the lines to reach the stars at the glamour positions were long. Quarterback Chad Henne. Receiver Steve Breaston. Even freshman running back Kevin Grady, who had yet to play a down, had his queue.

The scoreboard clock was ticking; 75 minutes left for Fan Day.

Most freshmen were easier to reach. They were lined up in the north end zone. Only a handful would ever hear their names read over the public-address system as starters. But the cognoscenti who had shown up that day knew exactly who they were. The zealots had read the biographies on the web, followed the entire recruiting process. They could reel off their current place on the depth chart. Michigan football is the closest thing to a religious experience that many of them will ever know.

"Eugene Germany," the mavens said. "Transferred from Southern Cal last year and sat out the season. Supposed to be one of the fastest defensive ends in the country."

"Terrance Taylor," they said. "National wrestling and power-lifting champion. Third on the chart at nose tackle."

In a year or two, these young men might also be at a table on the sidelines with the crowds lined up for them. For now they stood in comparative anonymity, obligingly posing for a few photographs because they were the easiest ones to get to.

There were a few surprises. A player was signing autographs with his other arm in a sling. It was Tim Jamison, a defensive end. The cell phones came out as absent friends were notified of this revolting development. What did it mean?

Everyone already knew that the starting right tackle, Jake Long, counted on as a bulwark of the offensive line, had gone down with a leg injury in practice and might miss half the season.

At Michigan, everything builds from the offensive line. That was the mantra that Bo recited for more than 20 years, and if you went to his office over at Schembechler Hall, he'd tell you the same thing today. If you don't have an offensive line, you don't have anything.

Right tackle is the position that makes the Michigan running game go. The Wolverines always manage to find highly mobile 300-pounders for that position, and Long was the prototype. Now he was done for six or seven games.

Good grief, was it starting already?

In 2004 it had been a preseason shoulder injury to starting quarterback Matt Gutierrez. The only backup behind him was Henne, a true freshman. No freshman had started that position at Michigan since Rick Leach, three decades before. The bloggers were given over to despair and warned that this could be it; the Wolverines could be heading for their first losing season in 37 years.

Henne, instead, went 9–3, took the team back to the Rose Bowl, and looked as studly as a young Tom Brady.

Still, losing Long meant another key man down before the team had seen a single snap. Bad karma in Ann Arbor.

A large man in a white shirt, Michigan insignia on his chest, walked by, heading for the tunnel.

"Hi, Coach," called the cognoscenti. "Welcome to Ann Arbor."

The name was not yet familiar to most Michigan fans, but everyone knew why he was there. Steve Stripling was the new defensive line coach. A most interesting choice in that for the last two seasons he had filled the same job at Michigan State. Usually, there is not much movement between these two great rivals. But these were not usual times. Even the most casual Michigan fan knew that if the Wolverines were going to make a run at any kind of title, national or conference, something had to be done about the defense.

In the last four games of 2004 it went through a meltdown, giving up 132 points and losing twice. Defensive coordinator Jim Herrmann, hailed as a genius during the 1997 championship season, had become the most reviled man in the Michigan program—a guy who supposedly didn't have a clue about how to stop a running quarterback.

So the ex-Spartan Stripling was here on a rescue mission. His job was to figure out ways to put more pressure on mobile quarterbacks, keeping them contained both on

11

plays that were called for them and on scrambles. The true believers already were opening their arms.

"Welcome to Ann Arbor," they told him. And by the way, Coach, SOS.

Things were being given away on the field—posters, magnetized schedules, souvenirs. The lines were growing longer. The clocks were winding down.

And then the rain returned with a thunderous volley. Those who had been watching the black clouds roll in had already scrambled up into the stands and were making the 60-row ascent to shelter. The unaware were getting drenched.

"This is the conclusion of Fan Day," said the PA announcer, almost redundantly.

There was almost an hour left on the clock, and most of the people in the lines still didn't have the autographs they craved. But enough was enough. No one on the Michigan football team was going to court pneumonia by being out in that downpour any longer. Don't tempt the karma.

The fans understood, even if their day had been terminated.

We managed to return to the car with a minimal drenching. As we drove past the Revelli band building, however, we could see that the entire marching unit was still out on their practice field. They had formed the block M and were rehearsing "The Victors." The rain was pelting down, but they never broke formation. The football team may run for shelter, but band members are made of hardier stuff.

We continued to Angelo's and had our French toast. We deserved it. It had been a fine morning.

One week to the opener, and Northern Illinois.

How The Big House Grew

In the locution of the late play-by-play radio announcer Bob Ufer, Michigan Stadium was "the hole that Yost dug, Canham carpeted, and Schembechler filled."

But it remained for ABC's college football specialist, Keith Jackson, to call it "The Big House." He described it as the "finest place to watch a college football game in America." At his last game at the stadium before his brief retirement, Schembechler presented Jackson with a Michigan warm-up jacket. "The Big House" was enscripted on the back.

Jackson, who now does network games on the West Coast, can't recall how the name originated. On the one hand, it's pretty obvious. At its opening in 1927 The Big House was the largest university-owned football stadium, and it retains that distinction almost 80 years later. Somewhat obsessively so. All another university has to do is announce plans to add more seats than Michigan's and out come the architects and contractors to maintain the edge.

There was one lapse. Tennessee sneaked its capacity ahead by 90 seats in 1997. Cut to the quick, Michigan immediately broke ground for 5,000 new spaces to reclaim the lead.

It was not only size that excited Jackson's admiration, though. It was turnout. There have not been fewer than 100,000 bodies scrunched into those seats for a home game since 1975.

Open the gates and the seventh-largest city in Michigan rolls in, just about the same size as Ann Arbor's population on the days no game is played.

This is pretty much how Fielding Yost foresaw it. He stepped down as coach after the 1926 season to become athletics director. When he arrived at Michigan in 1901, the biggest home crowd of the season was 3,500 for a game against archrival Chicago. Michigan shut them out 22–0. In fact, Michigan shut out all 11 teams it played that year.

Although Michigan had played a sporadic schedule of between two and five games a season since 1879 and had become a regional power in the 1890s, the arrival of Yost and his "point-a-minute" teams marks the true beginning of the modern football era in Ann Arbor.

In those early years of the 20th century, colleges customarily scheduled major games off campus in expectation of bigger crowds. Not until 1904, in fact, did the Wolverines draw a five-figure crowd to Ferry Field. Again it was for a game against Chicago and during the team's historic 56-game unbeaten streak.

As enthusiasm grew, the crowds burst the bounds of the makeshift stadium. By 1920 big games were drawing 25,000 people, and when wooden bleachers were added the following year, the capacity went to 47,000.

It still wasn't enough. This was the decade in which sports went over the top. With the coming of radio, syndicated sports columnists, and a wave of unprecedented middle class prosperity, it burst its former bounds.

Babe Ruth and Jack Dempsey became national figures, and they were paid more than bank presidents, building stadiums on the force of their celebrity and attracting million-dollar gates. College football rode the wave. This was when Knute Rockne's Notre Dame squads became the first to be called America's Team. The Ivy League schools still played top-level competition, and famous New York sportswriters sent out thrilling descriptions of the big games at the Yale Bowl and Princeton.

From the Big Ten, Red Grange and Bronko Nagurski were names recognized all over the country. When they made their pro debuts, they delivered rare Sunday sellouts.

Yost was eager to get in on this growing interest. Moreover, Michigan's rivals already were building. Ohio Stadium was up to 70,000 by 1922, and Illinois soon was almost as big. Michigan had to keep up or else fall to a competitive disadvantage.

Yost wanted an entirely new stadium with a minimum of 80,000 seats, laid out so that it could be expanded to as many as 100,000 sometime in the future.

But his proposals were received skeptically by faculty and university officials. There was a growing backlash among academics toward this sports frenzy. Many of them wondered in good faith if it was not unseemly for Michigan to join it. Wouldn't it, instead, be a nobler stance to reject such spectacle and maintain the scholarly integrity of a great institute of learning?

The faculty senate tabled the proposal and formed a committee to study it. Usually, that is the kiss of death in a bureaucracy for anything that smacks of change. But Yost cannily turned to influential alumni to build support behind the scenes for his plan. When the committee, headed by business school dean Edmund Day, turned in its final recommendations in January 1926, the stadium was approved.

The university purchased a 16-acre tract of land along a slight grade between Main Street and the railroad tracks that ran behind Ferry Field. The cost was $239,000.

The architect was Michigan alumnus Bernard Green. He headed a Cleveland-based engineering firm that had designed Yankee Stadium and Detroit's Navin Field, as well as the football stadiums at Minnesota, Purdue, and several other universities. Even without the alumni connections, he probably would have been the best man for the contract.

It was determined that the most suitable plan for the site would be a bowl, with the entrance to the stands at street level and the playing surface 50 feet below. It was modeled after the Yale Bowl. But instead of an oval, the sideline stands were placed parallel to the field and, therefore, closer to it.

This was still semirural land in the mid-1920s, and much of it was swamp. So when work began in September 1926, the builders ran into trouble almost immediately. The high water table and underground springs flooded the site. Pumpers borrowed from the Detroit Fire Department had to be brought in, and even with water being removed at the rate of 60 gallons per second, the flow could not be contained. Finally it was decided to raise the playing surface by six feet, and that seemed to remedy the problem.

Total cost for excavation and drainage was $33,000 more than the land acquisition price. But by May 1927, concrete was ready to be poured. That process went on for four months. Then sod was laid, benches installed, locker rooms finished, and, miraculously, just a bit more than one year after the work had begun, Michigan Stadium was completed within budget.

This was "the hole that Yost dug." Total cost: $1.1 million.

It seated a good 5,000 fewer than Yost had wanted, but he got around that by installing another 10,000 bleacher seats on the upper concourse, bringing the actual capacity to around 85,000.

The opening was October 1, with Ohio Wesleyan as the opponent. But the crowd of 17,483 could easily have fit into the older version of Ferry Field, and so could the next week's crowd for the game against Michigan State. Fans had been scared off by stories of construction problems. Yost knew, however, that the advance for the other three home games— against Ohio State, Navy, and Minnesota—indicated sell-outs. So he delayed the official dedication until the Ohio State game three weeks later. The season finale against the Gophers (OSU didn't become the traditional closer until 1935) established a record of 84,423.

That record would be eclipsed by the 1929 Ohio State game, when 85,088 came into the stadium.

Now that Michigan had its Big House, however, the problem for the next 45 years would be how to fill it. The supply of seats was finally there. But only rarely was it equaled by demand.

Yost couldn't have foreseen the Great Depression and World War II, two of the most powerful crowd suppressants imaginable. Only once in the next 16 seasons did attendance ever reach those early levels. Only 10 times in that period were there as many as 70,000 in the stands.

Through three undefeated seasons and the great Fritz Crisler teams led by Tom Harmon, Michigan remained a national power. On many dates, however, the stadium was less than half full, and Michigan was consistently outdrawn at home by OSU. That was the canker that gnawed at Michigan.

But as postwar prosperity came rushing in, so did the fans. It helped that the surge coincided with another of the great eras of Michigan football. Crisler's undefeated 1947 team, "the Mad Magicians," and the 1948 national champions, coached by Bennie Oosterbaan (captain of the 1927 team that had inaugurated the stadium), drew consistent sellouts.

So in 1949 the stadium got a little bigger. Yost's bleachers, still standing after 21 years, were removed and permanent seats installed. That added another 12,000 seats overall, and The Big House was now at 97,000. Five out of the six home games drew more than 90,000 fans that year, setting an NCAA attendance record.

Unfortunately, Michigan football was about to enter the longest lull in its history. In only 11 seasons since the arrival of Yost had the team finished with a losing record. But seven of those seasons fell between 1951 and 1967. Michigan went to the Rose Bowl only once during that span. Its profile fell below that of Michigan State, which had joined the Big Ten and become a powerhouse, winning two national titles.

Stadium capacity was expanded again in 1956, but this was more a matter of symbolism than need. On October 6 a crowd of 101,001, the biggest in history at any college stadium, watched Michigan get snuffed 9–0. The snuffer, infuriatingly, was Michigan State.

The only visiting teams capable of filling the stadium were Michigan State and Ohio State—and not even every year. Nationally ranked teams failed to draw more than 70,000. On most Saturdays a ticket was available to anyone who walked up to the booth. If the weather or the team turned foul, the fans just stayed home.

This was the situation Don Canham inherited when he was named athletics director in 1968. A former Michigan track star turned businessman, he knew all about moving product. The thing was, he had an awful lot of it to move.

In his first year as AD, despite the fact that Michigan had an 8–2 team, there was an average of 33,000 empty seats for each home game.

One of the first things he did, as Ufer pointed out, was to carpet the field with Tartan Turf. But that was mere cosmetics.

Like most great salesmen, Canham knew that he was selling the sizzle as much as the steak. Michigan football was supposed to be above the crass considerations of the marketplace. Didn't the game sell itself? Wasn't that enough? In truth, however, the game at Michigan was strangling in its own aloofness, failing to draw a mass audience that might have no connections to the university but was eager to back a winner.

Canham saw that the action in 1968 was in Detroit, where the Tigers were on their way to a world championship. He hired airplanes to circle the ballpark, carrying banners advertising Michigan football.

Then he went to direct-mail campaigns, ads that emphasized the fun of a family outing at the stadium. The tailgates and pageantry were placed on an equal footing with the game itself.

Still, none of that would have worked had it not been for the one other change Canham installed: going outside the Michigan system for the first time in 30 years and hiring Bo Schembechler as head coach.

The 1969 upset of Ohio State changed the course of Michigan football. There were 300,000 people in the stadium that afternoon, if all the people who remember being there actually were. (Even the actual count of 103,878 was a record.)

The game signified a reversal of fortune not only on the field but also in the stands. However, attendance didn't shoot up all at once. During the next five seasons there were still a couple of November crowds below 70,000, even as the team went 50–4–1. But the increment was steady. Every year, the average climbed, up through 80,000 a year.

In 1974 the Navy game drew 104,000. That was something of a milestone, the first time ever that a six-figure crowd had come out for a game that involved neither MSU nor OSU. The average for the season was 95,000. The Big House had grown very *big* indeed.

Other things were going on in the state, too. The major pro teams—the Lions, Tigers, Red Wings, and Pistons—were all in eclipse through the 1970s. Not a single pennant among them. Although Michigan State won the NCAA basketball tournament in 1979, its football program was in a down period. So Michigan football was not only the best game in town, it was pretty much the only show worth seeing.

In 1975 four of the seven home dates went over 100,000. Starting with that year's Purdue game, on November 8, a Michigan crowd has never dropped below that number.

With the additions of 1997, the official seating capacity of the stadium is 107,501, although for most dates the announced attendance is more than 110,000.

It may be argued that once you get over 90,000 or so, the crowd looks pretty much the same no matter where you go. So Michigan Stadium doesn't look much different on a typical Saturday than a game at Penn State or Tennessee or Ohio State.

That is only what the eye sees. The mind knows that this is The Big House. Even if it's a matter of just a few thousand more faces and voices than the rest, that knowledge transforms it into something more.

When plans were announced early in 2005 for a $200-million construction program, including enclosed club seating, the configuration would have reduced total capacity by as much as 6,000. There was such an uproar that the university backed off almost immediately.

"That has been a really clear message we've gotten from our fan base," said Dr. Mike Stevenson, executive associate director for athletics. "Whatever we do, we have to maintain the present capacity. That is the direction we've been going."

Athletics director Bill Martin contends that some things will have to change, however. There's no getting around the addition of luxury boxes. "It's going to change because it has to," says Martin. "There is no way you can get around it [building luxury boxes], unless you dug the hole deeper and rebuilt the whole thing—and that's not going to happen. We have to make sure that the architectural style is consistent with a college environment, not a professional team environment. There is a difference."

Every survey indicates that keeping the stadium's designation as The Big House outstrips every other concern—even if it means narrower seats and crowded aisles.

"This is a critical, critical pride issue," says Stevenson. "We've got the largest stadium in America, and our fans want to keep it that way."

September 3:
Michigan 33,
Northern Illinois 17

s the Michigan band took the field, Bob Honchar crossed himself.

Sitting up in row 68 of section 43, high above the 25-yard line, he closed his eyes as he made the religious sign.

"I had to say a prayer because it is such a blessing to be here," he explained.

"We don't respect what we have. We are free, Ann Arbor is beautiful, the traditions run deep. I'm an old-fashioned Catholic, and I believe in living with honor and living with tradition. So I pray out of gratitude for all that."

Honchar's was a distinct minority opinion, though.

On an absolutely flawless September afternoon, at the start of a new season, against a spirited opponent, with the fourth-largest crowd ever to watch a Michigan home opener, the fans left The Big House grumbling.

Grumbling about the team's play has become as deeply embedded among Michigan traditions as the marching band playing "The Victors."

The final score was 33–17, a comfortable enough margin against a Northern Illinois team that figured to contend for the Mid-American Conference title.

True, the spot was 18½, but Carr famously eases up on outgunned opponents in the second half when he thinks he's in control. Besides, their coach, Joe Novak, was an old friend.

None of this sounded persuasive to the multitude. They only had to look up at the electronic scoreboards to see that Northern had run up 411 yards in total offense, more than 200 of which were on the ground. This was immediately interpreted as a catastrophe. This was not the dominating defense they had come to see. This was 2004 redux.

Oklahoma lost to Texas Christian today. Auburn's winning streak ended. Ohio State gave up 14 at home to a Miami (Ohio) team that generally was rated not as good as Northern Illinois.

It made no difference. To the bloggers and talk-radio mavens and the departing throng who walked back to their cars in the cool of the evening, this was the first quavering step of a journey into fear.

"You take away the one 74-yard touchdown run they made on us, and it wasn't a bad day for our defense," Carr patiently explained. (Editor's note: It was actually a 76-yard touchdown.) "Other than that, we gave them just a field goal and a very late touchdown and about 130 yards on the ground."

Free safety Ryan Mundy, who got himself sealed out of position on the long run, had been immediately pulled from the game, however.

The coach said he had accomplished his primary goals. Northern Illinois was forced to play from behind all the way, which is what you want against a team that relies on a running game. The offense, at times, looked unstoppable. Receiver Jason Avant had shown the sort of third-down playmaking that Braylon Edwards had given them for the last few years.

Most of all, aside from a handful of downs, Michigan played a very basic defense for the entire game. They had shown almost nothing that Notre Dame, coming in next week, could seize upon.

So for Carr the day had gone just fine, thank you very much.

And then he saw the films. Uh-oh! After that viewing he announced that there would be shake-ups on the entire front seven, and if they didn't play with a higher degree of physicality, he would find some players who would.

Carr is not a man who is stuck on stupid. Although he claims not to hear the discontent, in reality he hears it loud and clear, and sometimes, when it is still early enough to make changes, he even will do that.

It was, in truth, a splendid opener on most other counts. The 3:30 PM kickoff tended to spread out the incoming traffic a bit more than a noon or 1:00 PM start. Driving into Ann Arbor for a Michigan game can be an exercise in frustration.

Every ticket holder has a "secret" route to get from the freeways to the stadium with a minimum of aggravation. The most skilled know side streets that appear on few maps, and guests are sworn to secrecy about revealing details of the trip. It's a wonder the drivers don't require blindfolds.

Maybe 20 percent of the crowd will be made up of students who do not have to drive. The rest will be threading their way through the city's narrow business streets to find a favored parking space in a lot or on a front lawn. A good many of these spaces have been reserved and prepaid for years.

The Victors noticed right away that the Champions' parking lot had grown exponentially. That forced the Victors to find a space in a substantially reduced area. They also saw that there were plenty of empty spaces in the Champions' lot. They ascribed this to base motives. Dig a little deeper, the university seemed to be telling them, and you too can park in roomy convenience.

But that situation could not mar the festive air of the occasion. The good season was renewing itself once more. The tailgates and barbecues. The Frisbee and football tossers.

The Michigan sweatshirt may now hide a potbelly. Children have become grandparents. But here, as they prepared to enter The Big House once again, all is still as it was.

From the same old gang at the tailgate to the band's pregame routines to the public-address announcements that precede the opening kickoff, the day must be as constant and unvarying as the stars. They demand no less here.

There was one change, although only the most discerning could have detected it. Howard King was absent.

The PA voice of Michigan football since 1972 was in a Traverse City hospital recovering from surgery.

King is as cognizant of the meaning of The Big House as any man alive. His respect for tradition is deep and reverent. Although he has made the opening announcement something like 150 times, he still keeps a printed sheet in front of him so that it doesn't change by a single word.

"Good afternoon and welcome to the University of Michigan Stadium for this, the first meeting between Northern Illinois University and Michigan."

This time it was Carl Grapentine, who usually handles the announcements of the band routines, who was saying it. But only the most avid fan would have noticed the change.

King is famous for fretting over the pronunciation of players' names. "Grown men cry when they hear their son's name being announced as playing for Michigan," he says. "I owe it to them to get it right."

He goes right to the source, too. Early in his tenure in the Michigan press box, he saw one name that puzzled him and went to Schembechler for the right pronunciation.

"A few weeks later, this kid saw me and asked me to pronounce it a different way," says King. "I told him that it's how Bo told me to do it. 'I know,' said the kid. 'Bo's been doing it wrong, too, but I'm afraid to tell him.'"

A tradition that even antedates King's arrival was the announcement of the Slippery Rock State College score. It was always greeted with applause and laughter and had become part of the regular midgame routine.

"The year I got here, though," King recalls, "we subscribed to a new score service, and it just included the major schools. I tried calling the Slippery Rock press box a few times, but you couldn't always get through. What did I do? I hate to admit it, but a few times I just made up a score. Who would know?"

Now the out-of-town scores are posted on the scoreboard, and the Slippery Rock announcement has faded from Michigan lore. It's one of the few things that has.

The stadium at Northern Illinois is called the Dog House. That is because the football team is known as the Huskies. The arena is about 30 percent of the size of The Big House. In a town like DeKalb, Illinois, though, that's plenty big enough.

In recent years, because of the abject screwiness of the Bowl Championship Series selection process, Michigan has shied away from taking on dangerous opponents in its nonconference schedule.

In the mid-1980s, when the ultimate goal was the Big Ten championship and the Rose Bowl, you'd find Florida State, Miami (Florida), UCLA, or Washington on the schedule, along with Notre Dame. Although Notre Dame remains, the other teams are far more often the caliber of Rice or Houston or San Diego State—almost certain wins for Michigan.

Rarely are two top nonconference opponents scheduled, and when Michigan has gone on the road to play them, it has lost every time since the 1999 season. This tends to put a big crimp in their national hopes before conference play even begins.

So Michigan has discovered the MAC. Every year of the new century, one or more teams from this conference have been invited to The Big House. This is a fine and neighborly thing, because it means a big payday for the three state schools in that conference. Some of them can even stay in the game for a half before Michigan's deeper talent and bigger line begins to wear them down.

The university understands that these are not exactly marquee attractions, and accordingly it lowers ticket prices by 10 bucks for these games. Even downgraded in this manner, it is still a great experience for the fans of teams such as Northern Illinois when they make their first visit to The Big House. "Think of playing a perfect round of golf on the most famous course there is," said Bill Lundberg, as he stood outside the stadium for the first time. "That's how I feel about going in there."

DeKalb is located about an hour west of Chicago and about a five-hour drive from Ann Arbor. It has played on the road against Big Ten teams before and, the week after this game, would do it again at Northwestern.

But Northwestern is not The Big House. Not by a mile.

So one of the largest contingents of Husky fans in memory, more than 5,000 by some estimates, made the 300-mile drive east to follow their team. This was a once-in-a-lifetime road trip for most of them. Wearing bright red sweaters, they were easy to spot. They occupied the usual visitors' section in the south end zone, as well as a thin stream of seats that ran from the top to the bottom of the stadium in the opposite goal area.

Lundberg, a retired business manager at NIU, used some local connections to get seats near the 15-yard line.

"No one told us that they were right behind the band, though," he said later. "Great band. Maybe the best I've ever seen. But we were on our feet the whole three hours plus. When they announced a media timeout, everyone else groaned, but that was the only time we got a chance to sit down."

Back in DeKalb, Lundberg had a chance to reflect on the total experience.

"I knew it was going to be big," he said. "Everyone knows that. But what I wasn't prepared for was the sense of being so close to the field. The space has been maximized for spectators. You just feel that you're right on top of it, and for a stadium of that size, I thought that was a remarkable thing. I've been in much smaller stadiums where the seats seemed to be much more distant from the field.

"The other thing was no outside advertising. It seems every stadium you go into now, there are companies with big billboards in there. We do it in DeKalb—a bank, a medical center—because we need the revenue. But here it is just a pure college football experience. You know that you're in an upper echelon kind of place. Nothing is allowed to interfere with that.

"Everyone we met was so nice, too. Part of that, I think, was because they were pretty sure we were going to lose. But at the end they gave us a measure of respect. They saw those 400-plus yards on the scoreboard and watched that 76-yard touchdown run, and they realized that they had been challenged. And when they saw my red sweater as we were leaving, people went out of the way to tell me that. I thought that was exceptional."

Another hallowed Big House tradition is to jeer when the PA announcer requests a "warm Michigan Stadium welcome" for the opposition, and once again when he says the Michigan band will play the visitors' fight song.

"I wish they wouldn't do that," said longtime season-ticket holder Sandy Gelman from his seat, down the row from the prayerful Honchar. "It's a cheap gesture, and it has the effect of cutting down the intimidation factor. The other team hears it and they recognize that it's not hostile, that it's meant as a joke. So why do it?"

"Didn't even hear it," said Lundberg. "Must have been the student section."

In the Associated Press poll, meanwhile, Michigan has risen from fourth to third. What do those voters know that the Michigan faithful don't?

Thursday, September 8

There is no questioning Jim Herrmann's maize-and-blue bloodlines. He is Michigan to the core, in his 16th year as a member of the staff of assistants.

Herrmann was a three-year letterman at linebacker and played for Schembechler's first Rose Bowl champions, after the 1980 season. He'd grown up in Dearborn Heights, in the western suburbs of Detroit, barely a 30-minute drive down I-94 from the Ann Arbor campus.

After graduation Herrmann spent two years coaching high school football in the Detroit area at Notre Dame in Harper Woods and at highly regarded St. Mary's in Orchard Lake.

But the call of Ann Arbor was too strong. He returned in 1986 to spend four lean years under Schembechler as a graduate assistant and volunteer coach. When Bo retired and Gary Moeller was named head coach in 1990, one of his first full-time hires was Herrmann. He was made responsible for the inside linebackers.

Carr added special teams and the entire linebacking corps to his portfolio and, in 1997, his third year as head coach, promoted Herrmann to defensive coordinator.

It may be safe to say that no assistant coach in college football has ever made the impact that Herrmann did in that first year. His attacking defense keyed the national championship team, and he was named Assistant Coach of the Year.

Much of that originated with Herrmann's enthusiasm. He had a knack for getting the players to sign on to his schemes and learn to trust each other. When his defense stifled Colorado 27–3 in the season opener in a game that had been rated little better than a toss-up, he could see his ideas coming together.

"The kids were like 'Wow,' coming off the field after every series," he said. "You could see the wheels going in their heads: 'Hey, if we do what we're supposed to do, this is what's going to happen.'"

"Right from this game our defense caught the imagination of the fans," said Carr. "Our crowd adopted that defense. The team fed off the enthusiasm in the early games at home."

The Big House was rocking. It suddenly had turned into a snake pit for visiting teams who were accustomed to playing there in an atmosphere more reminiscent of a public library. It was alive as it hadn't been for years, and it was mostly Herrmann's doing.

The key was constant, unrelenting pressure on the opposing quarterback.

Charles Woodson, who had been recruited by Herrmann and would come off that defense to win the Heisman Trophy (although several big plays on offense and special teams helped, too), said that the mood had been established from the first day of practice.

"We kept telling each other that we wanted to be vicious, to hit their quarterback hard and stop them all," he said.

"The defense wanted to make things happen. Anytime a quarterback faces pressure like that, sooner or later he's going to throw some bad balls."

"There is no better feeling than attacking, blitzing," said linebacker Sam Sword, one of Herrmann's prize pupils at the position he understood best and later a graduate assistant under his former coach. "That was the mentality. Get after them.

"But you can't play that way unless you believe in each other. Every man has to know that everyone else is going to do his job. We had to stick together to make it work, and Jim gave us that confidence. The best was when the quarterback was convinced another blitz was coming and we'd drop back into zone. That's when we knew we had him. You could see it in his eyes. He didn't know what was coming next."

Michigan stifled every offense it played. Even against Iowa, when the Wolverines trailed 21–7 at the half—more points than it had given up in any three of its previous games—the defense stood firm. One of Iowa's TDs had come on an interception, another on a punt return. In the second half, the Hawkeyes were throttled with a field goal, while Michigan put up three touchdowns to win 28–24. It was the scariest game of the season. But it also proved the team was capable of playing from behind on both sides of the ball.

"Our kids grew up in that game," Herrmann said later. "They never lost their composure. It was 11 winged helmets knocking the hell out of somebody, flying to the ball, doing whatever it took to get it back."

But from his seat high above Michigan Stadium, the old coach was taking notes. Schembechler watched in approval as the defense controlled the game. This was the game he liked. Strip the opponent of his weapons and then turn the ball over to a low-risk offense.

He had circled a date on his schedule, though. It was the Wisconsin game, the week before Ohio State and played in Madison. He respected Barry Alvarez as a football mind, and he knew that the Badgers coach saw the same things in Herrmann's defense that he did.

"When you commit your end and your outside linebacker to the rush, that leaves only an inside linebacker to cover the quarterback and the trailer on the option," said Schembechler. "There's no backup. A good option quarterback can hang that guy out to dry."

That's exactly what Wisconsin tried to do, and the game turned into a battle for ball control. The Badgers, using the option, put together repeated long drives, some of the most sustained that Michigan gave up all year. They were within a touchdown late in the second half. But the Wolverines, using a short-pass offense led by Brian Griese, managed to hang on, 26–16. Most of the players called it the most physical game they were in all year.

Alvarez would go on to take this team to the next two Rose Bowls. During the off-season, however, the films of his offensive game plan for Michigan circulated widely. Close attention was paid, particularly at Notre Dame and Syracuse. In the first two games of 1998, Herrmann's defense was shredded by those teams' option quarterbacks, Jarious Jackson and Donovan McNabb. The defending national champions were torched on successive Saturdays, 36–20 and 38–28. And the Herrmann mystique slowly began to unravel.

Michigan had given up only 114 points in the 12 games of the championship season, a figure that would be exceeded by 100 percent in every subsequent season but one.

Offenses had opened up more throughout the Big Ten, and there was more scoring across the board. But the Wolverines were suddenly showing an unnerving tendency to give up more points than their own usually potent offense could score.

They ran up 31 and 29 against Michigan State and Illinois on consecutive weeks in 1999 and lost both times. That lapse cost them an undefeated year in Tom Brady's best season. There was the semilegendary 54–51 loss to Northwestern in 2000 and the 45 points given up to Tennessee (Michigan's worst bowl loss ever) in the Citrus Bowl following the 2001 season. In 2003 they lost to Oregon, 31–27, and to Iowa, 30–27.

All of these losses preceded the 38–37 Rose Bowl defeat to Texas and seemed to indicate to many Michigan fans that the team no longer had the defensive schemes that could keep strong opponents with mobile quarterbacks off the board.

There had been a time when Herrmann was regarded as the likely successor to Carr. Not anymore. The storm had been rising for several years. But now it was approaching typhoon strength.

It appeared, however, that Carr was oblivious to the windy weather. To an increasing number of the faithful, it seemed that his loyalty to Herrmann had strayed across the line into stubbornness.

While loyalty is a commendable attribute, engendered at every level of big-time athletics, stubbornness is a ballbuster.

So come on down from East Lansing, Steve Stripling, to see what you can do with that defensive front.

But that's not where the greatest uncertainty seemed to lie for 2005. The defensive backfield had lost All-Americans Marlin Jackson and Ernest Shazor. Although every major news service in the prediction business ranked Michigan in the top 10 going into the season (as high as third, according to ESPN, and as low as 10th, per *Sports Illustrated*), the caveat was that failures in this secondary could be the team's undoing.

Yet it was precisely there that Michigan's true believers claimed to find their greatest hope of defensive coaching potential. Ron English was starting his third season as the defensive backfield coach. After a college career at the University of California, he had been an assistant at Arizona State for two stints totaling six years, gradually expanding his duties to include the entire secondary. He was also credited with expanding Michigan's recruiting presence in California. Two top freshmen, Chris Richards and Johnny Sears, were plucked away from Pac-10 schools when English used his contacts in his home state. (It helped that English happens to be Richards's godfather.)

Blogging debunkers claimed that English's reputation was inflated, that people loved him only because he was the anti-Herrmann. For some that was plenty good enough.

Oddly enough, in a preseason interview assessing the team's defense for 2005, English echoed something that Herrmann had emphasized eight years before. The defense had to learn to trust each other. That's what had been missing.

"When you start giving up plays," he said, "everyone tries to overcompensate. Once you start doing that, you don't have a defense. That's kind of what happened to us. We got away from doing our individual jobs as a secondary and got away from being accountable to one another."

He preached preparation and mental toughness. He seemed to be in line for something big; however, if his backfield collapsed on him, that something might have to be somewhere other than Michigan.

The criticism was milder for the other half of the coaching staff, but it was there. After the 45–17 Citrus Bowl pummeling by Tennessee, Carr retooled his offense. Tight ends coach Terry Malone was promoted to offensive coordinator in 2002, and he fashioned some of the flashiest scoring machines in Michigan history.

In Malone's second year the team averaged 35.4 points per game. That was the fourth highest average in the modern era, and the following year it was 30.8 points, good for 10th place. (The highest average for a Michigan team during the last 70 years was achieved by Fritz Crisler's final squad in 1947, which scored 39.4 points a game and finished second to Notre Dame in the polls.)

Although Malone got credit for opening up the Michigan offense, the irony is that he was also criticized for not opening it up enough. While other schools were running variations of the spread, Malone was content to stay within the confines of a traditional offensive scheme.

There were also those who claimed the real credit should go to Scot Loeffler, the quarterbacks coach Malone brought down from Central Michigan. Loeffler had been recruited as a player by Michigan, but a shoulder injury ended his career. He won a letter with the 1996 champions, but it was as a student-coach.

Over the next few years as a graduate assistant, he was credited with helping to develop Brady (with whom he remains close), Griese, and John Navarre.

"Scot was going to be one of the greatest quarterbacks Michigan ever had if he hadn't blown out his arm," said Brady's father, Tom Sr. "He took all that vibrancy and all of his enthusiasm and knowledge and poured it into people. He poured it into Tommy, he poured it into John Navarre, and he's still doing it today. Without Scot Loeffler, Tommy might be a stockbroker."

Mike DeBord, who was then Michigan's offensive coordinator, got the top job at Central Michigan in 2000 and took Loeffler with him. But two years later he returned to Ann Arbor.

When Matt Gutierrez went down before the 2004 season, leaving Henne as the starting quarterback, it was Loeffler who was in charge of bringing the untried freshman along.

"The philosophy around here has always been to do what the quarterbacks can do," he said. "Brady and Griese were here for three years before they had to take over. What we had to do with Chad on the fly was to take the package and reduce it significantly in order for him to compete."

Under Loeffler's tutelage, the freshman took Michigan all the way to the Rose Bowl and never appeared to be straining to do more than he could.

Still and all, Michigan's offense sometimes has the look of a rock guitarist trying to break out of a banker's body. Carr remains Schembechler's disciple and can never shake off the idea that the purpose of the offense is to get a lead and then minimize mistakes. This approach drives Michigan fans wild in an era in which a two-touchdown lead in the fourth quarter cannot be regarded as safe.

There was also the matter of play-calling in the red zone. *Predictable* is the kindest term for it. "Two runs, incomplete pass, field goal" is the other description.

For all that, though, it was conceded that offense was the strength of this team. It was deep, young, and fast. There were no worries there.

But the other part of the mix was the return of DeBord. He had been offensive coordinator in 1997, and Carr's loyalty to him for bringing home the championship was no less than it was to Herrmann. Behind Griese, a quarterback with limited skills but a great understanding of the game, he had fashioned an offense that did just enough to win.

When DeBord's four-year run at Central ended, he was brought back to Michigan in 2004 as special-teams coach. That may be the official title, but DeBord's real job is figuring out ways to get the ball into Steve Breaston's hands. That can be more difficult than it sounds, because after a brilliant freshman year as a return man, Breaston was injured for much of 2004. Attempts to use him as a receiver fell flat. But Breaston remains the wild card, a player who can break a game open at any moment.

DeBord, correspondingly, is the wild card on the staff. Close to Carr and with head-coaching experience, he is seemingly overqualified for the special-teams slot. The word is that Lloyd can hardly wait to move him back into his former position with the offense. If Malone should stumble, that's the scenario that will play out.

Stumble? With this offense? It hardly seems likely.

But the preamble is over now. It is September at last, Notre Dame is coming to town, and it's about to begin for real.

Friday, September 9

Get out the meat. Here comes Jaffe.

Eight pounds of salami. Twelve more uncut salamis. Eighteen pounds of corned beef. Twenty pounds of turkey. Twelve pounds of roast beef.

There are also 26 pounds of tuna, 20 pounds of smoked salmon, several dozen bagels, and 24 loaves of rye bread.

And this does not include the mixed drinks, the soft drinks, the ice and the packing materials, the cookies and cakes.

Every home game Ira Jaffe goes through this inventory of food and equipment. At 3:00 on Friday afternoons a large truck is backed up to his garage door in the suburbs of Detroit. A few minutes later a four-man crew comprised of security guards from a nearby apartment complex arrives to load it. Every container is labeled to speed the process, which takes just under an hour.

At 7:15 the following morning the truck will leave for Ann Arbor and the noon kickoff against Notre Dame. It will arrive 45 minutes later. By 9:00 AM the tents will be set up on a grassy incline next to the stairs to the stadium gate, and the food will be ready to serve.

From another point in the suburbs, Dr. Mel Lester will be sending his contribution. He makes the hot food. Hot dogs and chicken and a special dish he prepares personally for each game.

Last week it was linguini with clams. Today it is crabcakes. For Ohio State it is always beef tenderloin.

On a typical Saturday, around 600 people will feed at the Jaffe-Lester tailgate. Some of them will have been invited. Some of them will even know Ira and Mel. It is, far and away, the biggest party at the stadium and has become a Big House institution among its devotees.

Then next home game they'll do it all over again.

How long has this been going on?

"Too long," is the quick response from Jaffe's wife, Brenda. "I don't go to many of the games anymore. It's all a bit too much."

The correct answer is since the late 1960s, when Jaffe began bringing his mother to the games. Three of his nephews and nieces were attending Michigan at the time, and he thought it would be nice to set up a weekly tailgate so they could spend time with their grandmother.

"They asked if they could bring some friends, and I wasn't going to tell them no," he says. "And then it just kind of grew. Friends started showing up, and they had kids, and after a while their kids started having kids.

"Mel's tailgate was going in the same direction, and mutual friends began comparing what we were serving. In about 1982 we decided to combine. It got so big that the university was getting complaints that we were disturbing the people next to us. And that was true. So the university agreed to let us have this space, and we've been there ever since."

On this Friday, Jaffe has been awake since 5:30 AM organizing the material in his garage for the afternoon pickup. He even has built a loft with a drop-down step ladder to store more of the tailgate stuff. When the truck returns to his house after the game, it will take another hour to clean it all up and repack it for the week.

Why does he do it? With a very successful legal practice and having reached 65, the age when people traditionally start slowing their lives down, why does he keep it up?

"You wouldn't have to ask that question if you came down to our basement," says Brenda. So we descend the steps and enter a maize-and-blue universe.

Every single space in this area bears those colors. Walls, banners, blankets. It is a shrine, not only to Michigan football but to all its sports.

Here in a special case is one of the shoes Rumeal Robinson wore when he sank the free throws that gave Michigan the NCAA basketball title in 1989. Here are buttons from every bowl game in which the Wolverines have played: Fiestas and Sugars and Oranges and countless Roses.

"Go to hell, Auburn," reads one button. But is it from the 1984 Sugar Bowl (Auburn 9, Michigan 7) or from the 2001 Citrus Bowl (Michigan 31, Auburn 28)? Impossible to tell.

On one wall is a photograph of legendary receiver Anthony Carter lolling on a raft in the Jaffes' backyard pool. On another is a picture of a much younger Jaffe posed between Schembechler and Woody Hayes.

There are old action photos of Tom Harmon. A Bob Ufer bobble-head doll. A gross of autographed footballs bearing the signatures of Hall of Fame coaches and players. The only exception in this Michigan museum is a model train set up on a table for his grandchildren.

You would never guess from this display that Jaffe actually graduated from the Massachusetts Institute of Technology, where they do not, never have, and never will play big-time football. He does have a law degree from Michigan, though.

Brenda is another story.

"I started at Michigan State and graduated from Ohio State," she said. "Are you starting to wonder how we've been married for more than 40 years? Ira tells me that I'm still on probation."

But the legendary tailgate may be nearing its end—not through any flagging effort on the part of its sponsors, but because the university may want the land.

"You look at the plans for expanding the stadium, the private boxes and walkways, and it's pretty clear that it has to come out to where we are," he says. "If not in 2006, then certainly in 2007. So I'm pretty sure that either this season or next will be the last one for us. The one good thing about it is that it will make my wife so happy."

The loading is completed, and the crew members head back to their regular jobs. Will they be going to this game?

"Friday night's my bowling night," says Jerry, who leads the operation. "I'm pretty much dragged out by the time I get to bed at 3:00 in the morning. I can't get with these noon kickoffs. Besides, I think the November games are better for tailgating. Everybody's huddled together in the stands to keep warm. It feels good to eat a lot before you go in for one of those games."

Temperature at game time tomorrow is supposed to be in the 80s.

September 10:
Notre Dame 17,
Michigan 10

There is a buzz about this game. Any dolt can feel it on even the shortest walk through the streets of Ann Arbor.

It is much different than the sense of anticipation before last week's game. That was the opener, and there was no way Northern Illinois was going to win—not unless the earth opened up and swallowed the Wolverines as they ran from the tunnel.

But this week it's more than anticipation. There is also trepidation.

There always is in September.

This is a month that has been unkind to Michigan. Not since 1999 has the football team come into October unscathed. And in those five September losses, the total margin of defeat was 22 points.

Two of those losses were administered by Notre Dame, but they were both at South Bend. The games between these two teams are usually gut-grabbingly close. But last time the Irish came to Ann Arbor they were scalded, 38–0.

That only adds to the general uneasiness. Notre Dame doesn't forget whippings like that because…well, because it's Notre Dame. It carries a tradition as great as Michigan's, and, eventually, it must have its revenge.

Some hope that already happened last year when, in Henne's second game as a starter, saddled with an ultra-conservative game plan, Michigan never quite got on track and lost 28–20. That was the largest margin in this recent run of September losses.

That was not a good Notre Dame team. In fact, its coach, Ty Willingham, was fired. Now it is Charlie Weis, late of the New England Patriots, who leads them.

The Irish crushed Pitt, the defending Big East champs, in their opener. But that was ameliorated somewhat by the fact that Pitt went on to lose at Ohio. Major conference teams schedule Ohio to wipe their cleats. Unlike some MAC programs, Ohio is never a threat to upset anyone. But it just did, and that makes Notre Dame's opening cruise less ominous than it originally appeared.

Still, there is this sense that this first big game of 2005 is weighted with danger. An unknown quantity has come to town, and with that terrible Michigan defense everyone keeps talking about, who can say.

It is part of being a Michigan fan, however, to expect the worst.

So as the footballs fly back and forth across Greene Street, from the front porches of party houses to young women randomly chosen from the sidewalk crowds moving toward the stadium, the air can best be described as edgily festive.

"I even got invited in at one of those parties," says Gerry Mason. "That's never happened to me before. I was just walking down the street with my son, and they asked us to come on in. It was all very friendly. They introduced me to the frat president. It couldn't have been because they thought I was a candidate for rush. They were just being enthusiastic. It makes you feel good about the younger generation."

Mason is an attorney from St. Clair, Michigan, and was a Republican candidate for the university's Board of Regents in 2004—an unsuccessful candidate.

We are jammed into the line waiting to enter the stadium. The line is about 10 feet across, and the entrance is five feet wide. This presents a problem in physics. Things like this remind one that the basic infrastructure of The Big House is almost 80 years old. Much like other beloved stadia of another era—the Rose Bowl, Fenway Park, the Coliseum (the one in Los Angeles, not Rome)—many of the facilities are antiquated. So as we squeeze together, there is ample time to talk.

"I have a special feeling for this university," says Mason. "I went here as an undergrad, but it's more than that. I was born legally blind and spent some time in an orphanage when I was a kid. But I came to University Hospital for two surgeries, and they gave me my sight. How can you not love a place that does that for you?

"I've got two University of Michigan plates on my car, one in the front and one in back. That's the only way I'll drive. People say I'm a little excessive on the subject. And I say, 'Yeah, so what's your point?'

"See, I never got the chance to play any sports at all when I was young, let alone football. But I found that it's like family here. You get to know some of these former Michigan football players and they bring you right in. I've been asked to homecoming events with these guys. John Arbeznik...he was a captain on the 1979 team...is one of my closest friends. 'The Flame,' they called him, because he was so intense. Jamie Morris. Fred Jackson. These are really special people. Family."

Bob Ufer liked to compare Bo Schembechler to General George S. Patton, the brilliant tank strategist of World War II. When Michigan scored a touchdown, he would toot a horn in the broadcast booth that he claimed came from Patton's staff car. Mason likes the comparison, too.

"My favorite quote comes from Patton, in fact: 'Do not tell a man what to do. Tell him what you need and he will surprise you with his ingenuity.' That's what I believe."

Everyone seems to be sure what Michigan needs. It remains to be seen if the defensive ingenuity is there.

There does seem to be something odd afoot in Ann Arbor today. Too much afoot, in fact.

For many years, Michigan students were depicted as being smug—if not apathetic—about their football team. They came out in large numbers, and many of them traditionally stood throughout the game. But for a stadium of this size, The Big House has never been noted as an especially loud or unnerving place to play. There may be a sea of faces up in the stands, but most of them seem to have their lips sealed.

This year, however, the university is telling the students to get off their feet and sit the hell down.

The reason is that, like the demand for all Michigan tickets, student requests have reached record levels. They have overflowed the capacity of the usual student section in the northwestern corner of the stadium. So 2,000 undergrads had to be given seats in the south end zone.

Ten years ago the university sold only 14,000 student tickets. But after the national championship of 1997 it went to 20,000, and that number has inched up annually ever since. Some underclassmen could obtain tickets for only a few games, and there were bitter complaints. To make sure all students who wanted tickets got them, the university opened up this new section for them.

The seats were, unfortunately, right in front of some older ticket holders. Like their classmates across the way, these students chose to stand. The people behind them, however, preferred to sit. They regarded the student arrivistes as vertical interlopers. Shouting ensued and with it a few unseemly food fights.

So all student ticket holders in that section were sent emails by the athletics department suggesting, in effect, either sit your butt down or we'll throw it out.

"We understand that students stand as a part of culture," said associate athletics director Marty Bodnar. "We still want them to cheer—cheer hard and cheer loud."

The students involved approached the problem philosophically, in a manner befitting Michigan students.

"I'm a follower," admitted freshman Connor Brown, quoted in *The Michigan Daily.* "So if other people are standing, I'll do it. I'm not going to be the only guy standing, like a revolutionary."

It is probably good that Mr. Brown was not at Michigan back in the 1960s.

As things developed, however, there was not much reason to stand on this brilliant afternoon. The Michigan offense played one of its worst games in memory.

The unit that was supposed to carry this team collapsed in a pool of turnovers, missed reads, and injuries. Meanwhile the defense, the much-despised half of the Michigan team, was semi-superb. Aside from a 76-yard touchdown drive from the opening kickoff and a deflected pass caught in the end zone, the Michigan defenders were impregnable.

This confused everyone.

"Fire...give me a minute," started off one blogger who typically had demanded the head of Herrmann in most of his previous attacks. Who was he supposed to blame for this debacle?

"I think we found a defense," said Carr, smiling amid the rubble.

Nonetheless, the first two starters at right tackle were now down. So was tight end Tim Massaquoi. Right guard Matt Lentz was playing hurt most of the game. Running back Mike Hart left in the first quarter with a pulled hamstring, and his backup, much-touted freshman Kevin Grady, fumbled near the goal line for the second time in two weeks. The ball was recovered, but the failed play blunted an important drive. Backup wide receiver Adrian Arrington was out, too.

The injuries were unfortunate, but that is part of football. What disturbed the faithful much more was the almost total ineffectiveness of all-purpose back Steve Breaston. A threat to go off from any part of the field in his first two seasons, he seemed slower, tentative, unable to make the big plays.

Then there was Henne, who looked more like a sophomore than he ever had during his spectacular freshman season. Two critical turnovers, when Michigan had a chance to pull it out, crippled the Wolverines. He also seemed unable to complete his reads and find open receivers.

Maybe the worst sign of all was that many under the Michigan tent were blaming the officials. They claimed that Henne had broken the plane of the goal line on the play prior to his damaging fourth-quarter fumble. The officials, however, declined to order up a replay. But one play later, when the initial call was that he had not fumbled, the replay showed that he had, and Notre Dame recovered.

Winners run off the field leaping. Losers blame the officials. And the students throw plastic water bottles on the field. It was hard to tell, though, whether they were sitting or standing.

That play also touched off a major diaspora from the stadium. A fourth-quarter goal-line fumble can do that sort of thing.

Others had left even earlier, deciding to find a place in the shade at halftime and follow the game by radio or text message, or even trying to figure out what was going on from the volume of cheers inside.

It was much warmer than expected, with the temperature hitting the high 80s under cloudless skies. Although The Big House can be toasty in November with everyone jammed in together, it's less pleasant on hot September afternoons when such proximity to your neighbor seems one step removed from heat stroke.

Adam Breen was not complaining, though. He did not leave his seat until the final gun was fired. He and his wife, Jill, had planned this trip for months, selecting this game to fly in from New York. It had to be early in the year because Jill was pregnant, and by November that could have presented problems.

The trip took some planning, though. They secured accommodations at the Campus Inn on the first day its rooms were released, exactly 10 months before game day. Then they entered an alumni lottery for tickets, getting up at 6:00 AM to make sure their names were faxed in early. Ahh, but not early enough, as it turned out. They didn't get the tickets. Still, they came into town on the previous night, secure in the confidence that somehow, someway, fate would not deny them a way into The Big House.

"The first game I ever saw here was one of the worst in Michigan history," said Breen, a financial analyst who grew up in Atlanta. "I was visiting the campus in 1991 and got tickets to the Florida State game, when they ran up 51 points on us. But I was hooked. The whole scene, it was just more than I ever imagined. The electricity, babies and 90-year-olds, people coming here from all over the state. That's when I made up my mind to enroll at Michigan. The status of the business school was a big factor, too, of course, but The Big House sealed it."

The Breens' faith was rewarded. The father of a college friend came through with the ducats. Pretty good seats, too. Right on the 30.

"We'd been trying to get back there for five years," said Breen after his return to Manhattan. "But something always came up. My grandmother died, my daughter was born. Big things. So it wasn't through lack of effort.

"We convinced some friends to come with us, too. I love showing the stadium to first-time visitors. You just can't grasp how big it is from the outside. You know that it's a bowl, but you really don't understand what that means until you see it. Then you walk in and you see that you're entering all the way up at row 60. It's a stunning feeling.

"I've had the chance to see Michigan play since the last time I was here. We drove up to Syracuse one year from Manhattan, and when we were living in Chicago we went to games at Northwestern and Notre Dame. But there is nothing that compares to this.

"We met up with our friend after the game, and he told me it was awesome. The only thing he said that he regretted was that he didn't get to savor the true experience because Michigan didn't win.

"I told him that was the true Michigan experience. That massive letdown after they lose a game they should have won—that is something every Michigan fan knows."

As it turned out, even this well-planned weekend went awry. The Breens had planned to stay until Sunday, but they got a phone call from home—which can probably be described as the true parental experience—that their daughter was sick. So they rushed to the airport to catch the last flight out Saturday night.

"Worth the trip," said Adam. "Even with a loss and the short stay. Worth the trip."

The bloggers sized up the wreckage and predicted a 7–5 season. Coming in with your hands up at the first hint of adversity has also become a Michigan tradition.

Thank God it's only Eastern Michigan next week.

On the same day that Michigan fans were bemoaning their sad defeat, a visitor from out of state was watching his own team play on television. He wept at the sight.

Richard Lorenz lived in New Orleans and was forced to seek refuge with relatives from the floods loosed by Hurricane Katrina. His house was now filled with three feet of water, and a fallen tree had crushed its roof.

Louisiana State was scheduled to meet Arizona State in Baton Rouge that Saturday. But the city was so jammed with the sick and homeless of New Orleans that playing the game there was out of the question. So it was transferred to Tempe, and with a four-touchdown rally in the fourth quarter, the Tigers pulled it out.

"I was watching it, and I started to cry," said Lorenz, a psychotherapist. "You understand, it's more than just the game."

LSU football meant home, a home that had been lost to him, perhaps for good.

Maybe that's where the special appeal of college football lies. Unless you are actually an alumnus, loyalties seem defined by state lines, by home, far more so than with pro sports.

People in northern Florida, for example, will root for the Atlanta Braves, and in northern Iowa they tend to cheer for the Minnesota Vikings. But when Florida plays Georgia at the Cocktail Party, or it's Iowa against Minnesota for the

Floyd of Rosedale, there's no question about who they'll root for. They're for the home state.

Notre Dame is just a few miles across the Indiana line from Michigan. In the great days of the railroads, it was customary to alight in Niles, Michigan, and then take a cab for the short ride to the Notre Dame campus. But while an Indianapolis newspaper will assign a full-time writer to follow the Irish, almost no sports page in Michigan does so. The school is five miles too far south, in another place.

Hard feelings that originated deep in the American past are transmuted into college football games. Kansas versus Missouri is an echo of the bloody border wars of the 1850s. Then there's Oklahoma-Texas and Kentucky-Tennessee. When Virginia played West Virginia in a bowl game a few years ago and made slighting references to hillbillies during the halftime show, the West Virginia state legislature demanded an official apology. The two states haven't cared much for each other since West Virginia broke away during the Civil War to form a state of its own.

Michigan and Ohio nearly went to battle in the 1830s over ownership of the Toledo Strip. The ancient grudge is renewed each November, and the feelings are hardly any more cordial.

Watching the team from his home state in action, while both he and they had been flung far from home, was almost more than Lorenz could bear.

The feeling is far more diffuse in Michigan, which has two big-time programs within its borders. But in states like Nebraska or Arkansas—or Louisiana—the college game is the only show around. Years ago Tulane competed with LSU on an even playing field. They were both members of the

Southeastern Conference. In fact, one of the strange crusades Huey Long embarked on when he was governor of Louisiana in the 1930s was to build up the LSU football program so that it was on a par with Tulane. In his mind it was a matter of the people's school against the elitists.

Tulane is now a member of Conference USA, with a following that is far smaller than its former rival's. The two schools haven't even met since 2001, and the last time Tulane beat LSU was in 1982. Although Tulane's campus is located right in New Orleans and was inundated by Katrina, it is the program at LSU that has come to symbolize the state and can elicit tears from an expatriate.

In the face of great disasters, it is customary to say that such experiences put sports in their proper perspective.

But the truth may be just the reverse. The horror may actually be eased by an athletic team that summons up an image of the normal comforts of home.

4

September 17:
Michigan 55,
Eastern Michigan 0

This game is a dead spot on the schedule. Even the parking lot operators along Main Street know it. Their handmade signs all have a 0 as the second number of their price. They can change the first digit, however, with a flip card. Last week, for the Notre Dame game, it registered a 3. Thirty bucks a pop. Today the flipper has turned and a mere 2 shows instead.

Sure, the university drops its ticket price by $10 for the nonconference duds. But it's hard to see why parking lots do the same. After all, if more than 100,000 people still are going to show up, they have to leave their cars somewhere.

Chances are it won't be in the prepaid big-shot lots beside the stadium, either. Because this is the sort of game for which season tickets end up with office secretaries or lesser clients or second cousins or brothers-in-law.

Even making allowances for the quality of the opposition, there seems to be something else going on today. Northern Illinois was a MAC team, too, but that was the opener. Everyone gets up for the opener. Now, however, it's as if the air already has been let out of the season. Last week's loss has spread a pall over everything. The tailgates look sparsely attended, the house parties are flat, the buzz is missing.

Surely, all is not yet lost. Teams with one defeat do make the BCS title game. But the Notre Dame giveaway exposed weaknesses that were not supposed to exist on this team. All at once, the upcoming schedule looks ominous, dark, fraught with God-knows-what.

Besides, it's raining—a persistent drizzle that promises worse to come. The weather forecasters had promised partly cloudy and in the mid-70s, and most people had dressed accordingly. Now they are reduced to fashioning plastic rain gear from maize-and-blue garbage bags at the tailgates, punching out openings for their head and arms. It is not a pretty sight.

But the weather bags fit the prevailing mood. Garbage all the way.

The more despondent fans even murmur that Eastern's spread offense, the first of its kind that Michigan will face in 2005 after last season's disastrous experience, may give the Wolverines big problems. It may be a struggle. It may be worse.

Logically, that doesn't make much sense. Michigan has never lost to a MAC team, and if it ever does, it sure doesn't figure to be Eastern. Its Washtenaw County neighbor ("just 11 miles down the road but in a different world talent-wise," according to the sages at ESPN) occasionally comes up with a basketball team that can take the measure of the Wolverines. But there is no basketball being played at The Big House.

The schools have met six times prior to today, and in the first five meetings, the sum of Eastern's points totaled 0. The last time, in 1998, they got 20—and still lost by 39.

That game was played, in fact, in a situation quite similar to today's. Coming off its championship season, Michigan had been shockingly bludgeoned in its first two games, by Notre Dame and Syracuse. Starting with Eastern, it went on to win eight in a row and ended up in the Citrus Bowl with a 10–3 record overall.

So all is not lost, and David Lewiston, for one, refuses to lose heart.

After careful consideration, the Detroit-area attorney has selected a maize T-shirt for today's game, with "Michigan" lettered across the front in blue. He has a closet full of such apparel, and his game togs are a matter of deliberation.

"Not a great deal of deliberation, but I think about it just the same," he says. "Do I want to go traditional and wear blue with yellow lettering, or should I be a little bolder and reverse the colors? I'm not trying to send a message, but there should be some pattern, some coordination. Maize just seems more appropriate on a gloomy day."

On the back of one of his gym shoes it says, "Go," and on the other, "Blue."

"People know if they want to buy me a gift, this is what I want," says Lewiston. "It started about eight to 10 years ago, and after the championship year the fervor kind of gathered momentum. T-shirts, jackets, sweaters, sweatshirts. Some of it is dated and I never wear it anymore. After all, it's been a while since the championship. How long can you keep on wearing a shirt from 1997? People wouldn't stand for it. And a lot of that stuff just wore out.

"But I'm constantly replenishing the stock, looking for new ideas. A trip to Ann Arbor isn't complete without a stop at Moe's Sports Shop to see what new Michigan stuff they've got. At any given time, there are probably 100 Michigan articles in my closet.

"My feeling is if you want to wear these things, let them say something about what's important to you. Would I wear a T-shirt that says 'I Heart New York'? Certainly not.

"My wife accepts it in resignation," Lewiston says. "She just assumes that if we go anywhere, that's what I'll be wearing. Except to a formal wedding. Probably an informal one, too. There are limits.

"A few years ago we were driving to a game at Wisconsin with another couple. There was a blinding snowstorm, and it was ridiculous that we were even making this trip. Especially when someone pointed out that none of us had even gone to Michigan. But all our kids had. So there's the connection.

"I do have T-shirts from my old high school in Detroit, though. Mumford. Not nearly as many, but I wear them, too."

As they say at *Gentleman's Quarterly*, you are what you wear. But there are limits.

It didn't take very long for the Eastern Michigan matter to be disposed of. About four minutes, to be exact. Eastern completed its first pass out of the spread for 18 yards and an audible gasp escaped the crowd. But four downs later they punted, Breaston gathered it in, broke containment, and ran some 72 yards to the Eastern 10. A touchdown by Max Martin, who apparently had moved ahead of the fumble-prone Grady on the tailback depth chart, ensued.

After the kickoff, another Eastern punt was in order. This one was blocked, and Michigan was in business again at the 10. Once more, Martin was given the distinction of carrying it in.

With 30 yards of total offense, Michigan had a 14–0 lead, and it soon became much, much worse. It was 28–0 by the end of the quarter. The rest was commentary.

"I think the environment got to our kids," said Eastern's coach Jeff Genyk. Actually, it was a good deal more than the environment.

But there were some positive indicators. Henne got his groove back, and Gutierrez got some playing time. An injury-riddled offensive line filled with replacements got in a full game as a unit. Freshman Mario Manningham perked up the receiving corps. And a shutout is a shutout. Suddenly, the defense wasn't looking like that big of a problem.

So while 55–0 wasn't much of a test, it did settle the digestive systems of many people.

The game also netted somewhere around $300,000 for Eastern's athletic program. This is a very considerable thing, especially since the smaller in-state universities could not schedule a game in The Big House for more than half a century. Between 1943 and 1998, none were scheduled—and only wartime travel restrictions brought in Western Michigan on that earlier date.

As mentioned before, however, it is much too risky for teams with national aspirations to schedule two tough nonconference games. Only part of that can be blamed on the BCS bowl formula and the national polls. Back in the 1970s and 1980s, when the conference was much weaker and there was only Ohio State and maybe Iowa or Illinois to worry about, Michigan had no qualms about that sort of nonconference scheduling.

But the Big Ten is now a far more dangerous jungle. Since 1993, every team but Indiana, Minnesota, and Michigan State has won a share of the conference title. Only four times in those 12 seasons has Michigan lost fewer than two games in the Big Ten.

Almost every game on the schedule is a potential mine-field, and Wisconsin, Iowa, and MSU must all be encountered on the road this season. So step right into The Big House, Eastern, and we'll hold your coat for you while you're being slaughtered.

Even the Associated Press poll wasn't much impressed by this performance, though. Michigan started the day at number 14, and that's exactly where it finished.

Oddly enough, that was a few spots ahead of Notre Dame, which was upended at home by Michigan State the same weekend.

Figure this out if you can. Michigan loses to Notre Dame at home. But when the same fate befalls the Irish the following week, Michigan not only vaults back ahead of them in the poll, but both teams finish in front of undefeated MSU.

This is the sort of thing that makes the AP poll about as useful as martian algebra. The wire service says the BCS may no longer use it as part of its ranking formula. That probably goes under the heading of addition by subtraction.

The AP voters do not seem to live in the real world, where actual on-the-field results count. They seem to inhabit, instead, an imaginary plane of being in which decisions are governed by what should have been. It is also an existential sort of place, where the past disappears and only the most recent action has any meaning.

It must be so. Otherwise, how could Michigan finish ahead of a team with an identical record that had beaten them on their own home field just one week before?

The actual reason is quite simple. The AP voters are very busy people. They have a sports section to get out, a column to write, maybe a weekend radio or TV show to make an appearance on as a guest expert. They probably have time for only the most perfunctory glance at Saturday's results and will cast their vote on the basis of a familiar name or a regional favorite...or pure whim.

Some, of course, are quite serious about the whole thing, taking out charts and making careful comparisons before voting. Others give their vote to a copy boy.

Yet fans argue about these rankings as if they actually reflect something real.

The poll began in 1936 as a newspaper circulation gimmick, and Michigan has a rather checkered history in it. In the 1947 season, both Michigan and Notre Dame finished with perfect records, with the Irish ranked first. After Michigan's 49–0 blowout of Southern Cal in the Rose Bowl, however, the AP decided to hold an unofficial final ballot—since bowl results were not supposed to count. But that was like telling a jury to disregard a murder confession they'd just heard. The highly impressed voters gave Michigan the top spot, but in the official rankings Notre Dame went down as winning the national title. All the late poll managed to do was irritate fans of both schools.

In 1948, when both teams again had perfect records and Michigan was ineligible for a bowl, the Wolverines were named undisputed champions. Some would say it was a makeup call for the blunder of the previous season. Whatever.

Then in the notorious 1997 season Michigan finished the regular season ranked first in both the AP poll and the *USA Today* coaches' poll (which was originally instituted by United Press International in 1950). No number one team that won its bowl game had ever lost the top spot. But the coaches changed their minds and gave the title to Nebraska, while Michigan held on at the top in the AP vote. So for the second time a strange post-bowl voting switch caught Michigan in the middle. It was this strange contretemps that helped initiate the BCS, as a way of settling such disputes. As anyone can see, it has succeeded splendidly.

All in all, though, Michigan is usually overrated in these polls. There was no logical reason, for example, why the Wolverines started this season ranked at number four, except for the fact that they are Michigan. They appear on national television a lot, they always seem to win nine or 10 games, and they wear those terrific helmets. Everyone knows Michigan, and people tend to vote for a name they know, whether it's for a seat on the city council or in football. It would take some fairly catastrophic events to get them out of the top 25. If Northwestern had the exact same record at this point in the 2005 season, they wouldn't be anywhere close to 14th in the polls.

So the AP rankings mean nothing. Listen to Las Vegas. That's the only ranking that means anything. Bookies will clean out sportswriters every day of the week. They have already set the line for next week's game at Wisconsin as Michigan by three.

Sideshow

It is a strange anomaly that the most exemplary college football program in America is located about a one-hour drive away from what is arguably the worst-run franchise in professional football.

Yet on fall weekends the Detroit Lions also play to a sold-out stadium, and many of the seats at Ford Field are occupied by the same people who turned up at The Big House the day before. They may look on it as a form of penance. An overabundance of success in one place should be balanced by nearly continuous misery in the other. The Lions are the only football team whose fight song comes from the Book of Lamentations.

Going into the 2005 season, the Lions had been without a championship for 48 years. This dry spell was exceeded in the NFL only by the Arizona Cardinals. While the Cardinals have moved out of two other cities to clear out the stench, the Lions have been constantly fouling the same nest. Since their last title, in 1957, they have won a grand total of one playoff game, an absolutely remarkable achievement in a league that prides itself on parity.

This speaks volumes for either the loyalty or the stupidity of their fans. Probably both.

On this afternoon, when many forecasters thought the Lions would establish dominance in a weak division, they were absolutely plastered by the Chicago Bears, 38–6. Only the giddy could have been surprised.

As Michigan fans have learned to live with teams that seem to fall just short, Lions fans have become accustomed to teams that just fall all over themselves.

Still, they sell out the stadium. Of course, they have 50,000 fewer seats to sell than Michigan does. Even when they played at the Pontiac Silverdome, though, with a capacity of 80,000, they frequently drew a full house. Since the opening of Ford Field in 2002 every game has been a sellout.

A good many of these ticket holders bought in hoping to get lucky in the 2006 Super Bowl lottery. But after all the big shots were taken care of, the chances of that happening were infinitesimal, about the same as winning a real lottery.

Many Michigan fans are convinced, moreover, that there is a dark cabal directed against former Wolverines in the Lions' front office. True, Jeff Backus is a starter on the Detroit offensive line and James Hall plays on defense. But these are rare exceptions.

Fans point, instead, to the 1998 draft, when the Lions passed up Griese, who had just led the Wolverines to the championship, in favor of a frighteningly obscure Eastern Michigan quarterback, Charlie Batch.

Batch became another number in the long line of Detroit quarterbacks, stretching back to the era of Bobby Layne, who wouldn't do. Meanwhile Griese began this season as the starter at Tampa Bay, which won its first two games.

Even Carr didn't quite get that Detroit decision. But the ways of the Lions have baffled some of the best minds in football. It can be said with some fairness that throughout its ownership by the Ford family, whenever the franchise has had a chance to make a choice, it has been the wrong one. Through all the vicissitudes of this team, that ownership is the single constant.

When Detroit's other professional teams went into the tank, their fans stayed away to such a degree that it forced a change in ownership—or, at least, in direction.

But the Lions bumble merrily along, spreading desperation and horror through countless glorious autumn Sundays in Michigan, one wasted season following another.

Just an hour's drive apart—but, to paraphrase ESPN's comparison of Michigan and Eastern, a different world in management.

Wednesday, September 28

Dr. Peter Fugazzi steps out of his office to greet a patient who is wearing a shirt with a Michigan State insignia on the chest.

"You've got a problem there, my friend," says the physician. "A bird seems to have taken a shit on your shirt."

A spirited exchange of opinions ensues, the sort of thing that occurs between people who have been cheerfully insulting each other's football teams for years. But for Fugazzi, the cheer is a bit forced and his spirits are decidedly on edge.

He is a dedicated Michigan fan in the heart of Spartan country. His office is in Lansing, and he is about to buy a condo in East Lansing, right down the block from George Perles, the coach who took MSU to its last Rose Bowl.

"I'm a New Yorker, from the Bronx," says the doctor. "Do you need any more explanation than that? I talk funny. I've got to be different. It's part of my DNA.

"I've been hanging maize-and-blue banners in front of my house for 25 years. I've got Michigan posters, seat cushions, dolls in my office and in some of the examining rooms. Just enough to piss off the real Spartan fans. They take it in good humor. I wouldn't dare do something like that if my practice was in Columbus. They'd pull my license on me.

"But this week," he says, "they've been giving it back to me real good. It's starting to look like their time has come."

On October 28, 1967, Bump Elliott's Michigan team lost to Minnesota, 20–15. It was their fifth defeat, ensuring a losing season. The last one at Michigan.

How long ago was that? Lyndon Baines Johnson was president. Crowds were marching on the Pentagon to protest the Vietnam War. "To Sir with Love" was the most popular song on the radio. And $3 would almost fill a car's gas tank, instead of buying one gallon.

In other words, it was a very long time ago. But now the world has gone a little mad.

The Wisconsin game ended in a 23–20 loss. The Wolverines are 2–2 and out of the AP top 25 for the first time since the early weeks of 1998. They are in danger of being 2–3 for the first time since that dreadful 1967 season.

And, shockingly, for the first time since that season, MSU will go into this game as the favorite. That is far too many "for the first times since" associated with this game.

Now it is the Michigan fans who are reeling, trying to figure out what has gone awry, desperate to get the season back on track before it's too late.

The bloggers are going berserk. Up until now they have only demanded that Carr's assistant coaches be fired. But at this point they are circling around the head man himself.

Why is Michigan still running the same old tired offense, they want to know. Why isn't he out there hiring the next Pete Carroll or Urban Meyer, the sort of assistants who can put a little imagination and zing into their stodgy attack? How can Michigan keep getting the top recruits in the country and be 2–2 at the end of September? Has the game passed Carr by?

It feels as if the 1997 championship was a very long time ago—part of another century, in fact.

"I could tell that Doc wasn't feeling right about this game," says his nurse, Judy Van Vliet. "Usually he pulls into the parking lot with that song blaring from his stereo."

"'The Victors,'" says Fugazzi. "Don't call it 'that song.'"

"'The Victors,'" she says. "But this week when he drove up, you could hardly even hear it. And he's started saying things like 'I actually feel good for the MSU people.' It's very strange."

"Well, it's true," says Fugazzi, rather glumly. "This game is much more important to the State fans than it is to Michigan.

"I just hope," he says, with a glint returning to his eyes, "they can play up to their capabilities this Saturday. I'm tired of the bellyaching. They've got Michigan on the ropes. Get it over with. Run up the score. It'll be good for the rivalry. It would sure get Michigan's attention.

"If," he adds, with a pause for dramatic tension, "they can pull it off."

Indeed, even as Spartans fans prepare for a monstrous celebration, their lingering doubts cannot be entirely dispelled. There is still nervous apprehension, the suspicion that it just can't be this easy, the unshakable fear that Michigan will rise from the tomb and crush their expectations again. Because it's happened so many times already.

A headline on the *State Journal* sports page gives voice to such fears: "Scene Is Set for Big Disappointment."

It is ever thus in East Lansing, where Michigan fans are chippily referred to as arrogant asses. A big win over the Wolverines is not only a win on the field—it is a chance to rub the noses of their overbearing fans into the dirt. That would be the best part, the cream of the jest. At least, that's the view from Spartan Stadium.

There was a time when it all went the other way. Between 1950 and 1969, MSU's record against the Wolverines was 14–4–2. There was no question about which school was the dominant football team in this state. The most powerful radio station in Michigan, WJR-AM in Detroit, carried the Spartans games then. When the station switched over to Michigan in the mid-1970s, it was a key indicator that fate had turned, as did the loyalties of thousands of fans who had no affiliation with either university.

Since that 20-year period, which pretty much ended when Schembechler arrived in Ann Arbor, Michigan has dominated the series 27–8. In the 94 times the teams have met, MSU has won just 28 games—half of them in that pre-Schembechler burst of glory.

MSU coach John L. Smith even refused to call it a rivalry. "How can it be a rivalry when one team is so dominant?" he asked this week. Rhetorically, of course. This is only his third year in East Lansing, but he can smell a rivalry when it passes right under his nose.

Every one of those eight most recent MSU wins was regarded as an upset, and in some cases Michigan accused the Spartans of dastardly conduct in getting them. Things like putting some extra seconds on the clock so MSU could score a late touchdown at Spartan Stadium in 2001 and getting away with pass interference in the end zone in 1990 on a two-point conversion.

Arrogant asses, indeed.

Then there is the little matter of the 2004 game, when State couldn't hold a 17-point lead in the fourth quarter and lost in three overtimes. That one smarted worse than most. The Michigan band made a point of rubbing it in, too, during the halftime show of the Eastern game. It was intended as a spoof of the Broadway hit *Spamalot*, which is based on the film *Monty Python and the Holy Grail*. In the band's version, a character dressed as MSU's mascot, Sparty, was eliminated from the quest because he couldn't hold on to that lead.

The crowd roared.

But there is more than that, of course. Much more.

A typically mean-spirited Michigan joke: "What do all Michigan and Michigan State graduates have in common? They all were accepted at Michigan State."

State is a great research and teaching institution, and its graduates are not amused by such badinage. They are aware that Michigan ranks among the top two or three best public universities in America. But one monkey don't stop no show, as Motown reminded us many years ago.

The fact is that State is the more truly Michigan of the two schools, in its student body and on its football roster. Fully one-third of the University of Michigan student body comes from outside the state. Many of them are from absolutely insufferable places like New Jersey, Long Island, and the Bronx.

Like Fugazzi.

"No, I never went to Michigan," he says. "But my two sons did, and they married girls who have degrees from there. I actually came to Lansing for a residency at a local hospital, and I liked it so much, I stayed on. I was even on the faculty at State, teaching a course in family practice. I love this area.

"But I grew up a Yankees fan. I like winners. Michigan is always a winner. For me, going to their games is like attending a great concert. Some people like chamber music. I like a marching band playing 'The Victors.' I can drive down to Ann Arbor, go to a game, and act like a fool. It wouldn't be a good idea if my patients saw me acting that way in East Lansing.

"It was a bonding experience with my sons, too—something we could all talk about. Even today, when Michigan is on the road, they're on the phone with me all through the game, from Dearborn and Las Vegas, yelling about what the team is doing. My wife just leaves the house.

"But when I was out in Vegas with my son for the Wisconsin game, it was deadly. I knew I was gonna get it when I came to the office that first morning.

"You know what, though? On Sunday morning after the State game there will be 1.5 billion Chinamen who won't give a shit.

"Well, then again, maybe not. I was in Beijing a few years ago and walked to a newsstand, and there were Michigan T-shirts on sale. They're everywhere."

Some would say a bit too much of everywhere.

"I dread it when there's a night game with Michigan on TV," says the manager of a restaurant in the northern part of the state. "They sit in the bar, and they are the loudest, rudest, most inconsiderate people we get in here for any sport."

They had indeed come in for the previous Saturday's night game with Wisconsin, but the loudest sound was their groans of agony. To northern ears, it may have sounded vaguely like the call of an oversexed moose.

Michigan dominated the first half, although one possession left them stopped on downs at the 1, and just before halftime Carr chose to kick a field goal on third down rather than take one more shot into the end zone.

Still, the defense was solid, and going into the last quarter all the Badgers had on the board was two field goals. But longtime Michigan fans could see exactly what was coming.

Sure enough, Breaston, hearing music no one else could discern, tried to run the ball out of his own end zone on a kickoff. He got as far as the 8. A few plays later there was a fumble (hotly disputed, of course, by Michigan and its broadcasters); Wisconsin recovered and drove right in. They led 16–13.

But in its one sign of life in the second half, Michigan struck right back, with Grady faking a run and pitching back to Henne, who hit Manningham in full stride for the score. Michigan led again, 20–16.

They couldn't move when they got the ball back, however, and with about six minutes left in the game, they had to punt. And then, during the one part of the game in which the Michigan defense had to get off the field, it couldn't.

Wisconsin kept its drive going on two third-and-long plays. On third down from the 4, with less than a minute on the clock, their quarterback ran right in on a draw play. Turn out the lights. The party's over. The bar emptied out in the northern Michigan restaurant, and in Madison the beer began to flow.

It was a fond good-bye present for Alvarez, coaching his final season, never before having beaten Carr.

Any chance at a national title was gone. A third straight Big Ten championship looked highly unlikely. And suddenly this team was in the very un-Michigan-like position of staring at humiliation dished out by one of its biggest rivals.

"This is like waking up to find Fredo Corleone—not Michael—running the family business," writes *State Journal* columnist Todd Schulz.

"No matter what happens Saturday," says Dr. Fugazzi, "I will show up next week wearing my maize-and-blue tie. Even if my office is flooded with green."

He speaks like a man who is already steeling himself for the coming ordeal.

5

October 1: Michigan 34, Michigan State 31

ix-year-old Haley Wise walked into her next-door neighbors' house this evening and announced, "We're having blue pancakes tomorrow morning."

"You mean blueberry pancakes, honey," said her neighbor.

"No, they're gonna be all blue inside. If Michigan State won the game, they would have been green pancakes."

Her mother, Donna, explained later, "We have an interfaith marriage; I went to Michigan and Stuart went to State. We do the pancake bet every year. It's amazing what you can do to pancakes with a little food coloring."

As it turned out, the rest of the state, and not only the pancakes, are still blue. The real Godfather, and not his wimpy little brother, is still in charge.

Michigan is still Michigan. The planets are secure in their orbits. And the hopes of still another season have come down to smoke and ash in East Lansing.

"You remember when Kordell Stewart beat Michigan with that last-second desperation pass for Colorado?" asked Gordon Gold, one of the maize-and-blue faithful who made the trip to Spartan Stadium. "It was that same deathly silence when this one ended. Only worse."

"It was like somebody stuck a cork in the bottle," said Barry Bershad, another of the small corps of Michigan fans in attendance. "It was like somebody told 75,000 people that their mother had just died."

It was hard to tell how many Michigan people were actually there. A large contingent, maybe 3,000, was clustered in a corner of the end zone. But others were scattered throughout the stands, picking up stray tickets here and there. Knowing they would be isolated, most of them were wise enough to leave their maize-and-blue attire back in the bedroom closet.

"It wasn't that hostile, though," reported Gold. "In fact, it was kind of good-natured. We parked near some frat houses, and some of the kids were wearing T-shirts that said 'Maize and Who?' or 'Ann Arbor is a Whore.' That kind of thing.

"It was nothing like being in Columbus, where they spit on the players when they come out of the tunnel and they tell you to back your car into your space in the parking structure so they can't see the Michigan plates. Those people are sick."

"They were absolutely sure they were going to win," says Bershad, who was sitting squarely amid the Spartan horde, high in the third deck. "So it was really kind of a party atmosphere before the game."

It is just about 60 miles on the interstate, something less than an hour, to make the drive to East Lansing from Ann Arbor. Someone once wrote that the Midwest begins at the western city limits of Ann Arbor, because that city really looks to the East Coast in most things.

In East Lansing, though, there is no mistaking the region. This is a midwestern pastoral, the perfect evocation of the nation's heartland. Much of that sense is furthered by the rolling acres of experimental farms around the campus. State is among the top agricultural research institutions in the world.

Its central campus, with the Red Cedar River winding through its heart, is also distinctly different from the Gothic grandeur of Michigan's Quad. More accessible, somehow; or maybe *homier* is the better word.

But once more a shroud of gloom descended upon it after the fourth-straight loss to the despised Wolverines.

State has developed a nasty reputation for student frolics that get out of hand. There has been some couch-burning, car-tipping, bottle-smashing behavior after some games, win or lose, football and basketball, in recent years. The East Lansing cops put extra staff on its quelling squad for this game just in case the situation turned combustible.

They could have saved the overtime. Spartan fans were so crushed that they just went home, and Michigan fans riot only when they run out of brie. Besides, this one hurt too bad to play with matches.

"In the conversations I had with State fans before the game, the only concern was by how many points they were going to beat us," said Gold. "That was the issue."

"They were acting like Michigan fans are supposed to," said Bershad. "They were so sure, it was almost like arrogance. It was a complete reversal from what I'm used to in following Michigan. Usually it's us who come in as the favorites and lose."

In fact, you might have to go all the way back to the 1996 game at Ohio State for a comparison. That's when Griese came in as a sub and defeated the unbeaten Buckeyes, 13–9. That may have been the last time Michigan was such a big underdog on the road and won.

But this was not the same Michigan team that had taken the field for two out of the last three weeks. Something seemed to have clicked.

Some would say it was Carr's ability to use adversity as motivation. He waved off that suggestion, though.

"I didn't say anything that any coach wouldn't have said in the same situation," he said afterward. "Every one of these kids knew what was at stake."

Some would call it the Michigan mystique, the ability to summon up the will to overcome fearful odds by invoking the glorious past. But if the horses aren't there, that wagon won't haul.

The best explanation was that Hart had returned. Injured in the first half of the Notre Dame game and sidelined ever since, in this game he rushed for more than 200 yards. More than that, they were yards needed in critical third- and fourth-down situations—yards that his replacements had not been capable of getting when they had to. He seemed to hit the holes a step faster than they did and could not be tackled by just one man.

Michigan upset all the scenarios by jumping off to a 14–0 lead on its first two possessions.

"There was a family sitting in front of me, three generations of State fans," said Bershad. "The oldest guy in the group was getting so upset at State's conservative play-calling that he kept jumping up to yell about it. The kids kept telling him, 'Calm down, grandpa.' The funny thing was he was saying the same sort of things I usually say about Michigan's play-calling. It was part of this whole role-reversal thing."

But the Spartans came back and tied it up. Then they missed a gimme field goal, and then Michigan missed a gimme field goal, and in between all that, 300-pound Samoan lineman Donata Peko picked up a Henne fumble and rumbled some 74 yards to tie the game, 31–31.

For the second-straight year, it would go into overtime.

State, with the first possession, missed a three-pointer again. Then Garrett Rivas, who had just missed the game-winner a few minutes before, calmly kicked it through for Michigan on third down.

And a sickly silence roared through the stadium.

"After Rivas missed the first one, I couldn't take it anymore," said Bershad. "I started walking down through the stands, and when he was ready to kick again I was in the fourth row of seats behind those goal posts. Right in the middle of the MSU band. In the tuba section.

"When it went through, I started screaming, and then I realized I was the only one. I was getting some glares, and those tubas are pretty big. So I got out of there fast."

The Michigan band raced onto the field, and as the players gathered around they formed a bobbing mass at midfield. Two weeks before, some MSU players had kicked up a small controversy by planting a school flag on the turf at Notre Dame after upending the Irish.

Michigan simply stood in the middle of Spartan Stadium, playing and singing "The Victors." For MSU, that was infinitely worse.

Carr was almost in tears in the locker room. He told his team, "I'm already an old man, but I'll remember what you did today for the rest of my life."

He knew, more than anyone else, what this victory meant and how close his program had come to hitting the wall.

Maybe the most interesting aspect of the game, however, was the fact that MSU quarterback Drew Stanton did not hurt Michigan with his legs. He scored a rushing touchdown from close in, and his passing was effective. But in the 2004 game he was the first of the rushing quarterbacks out of the spread who drove the Michigan defense crazy at the end of the season. Running plays had been specially called for him in that game.

It didn't happen this time. Michigan's defensive containment on the run never broke down. Nobody was calling for Herrmann's head on a stake, and defensive line coach Stripling, the man who had come over from MSU, was quietly beaming.

October suddenly seemed a lot brighter. There was still something to win, something to hope for.

All the pancakes were coming up blue.

Saturday Morning, October 8

The topic of the day is loyalty.

When Joe Schmidt coached the Detroit Lions, he had a standard expression of contempt for front-runners.

"The boat is full," he would call out to the media as they trooped into the locker room. "The boat is full."

Meaning that a big win had brought all the doubters back on board for the ride.

Schmidt would also say things like, "Life is a shit sandwich, and every day you take another bite." But that hardly applies to Michigan fans, does it?

Still, it would have been forgivable had Carr revived Schmidt's old chant as the Wolverines prepared for Minnesota. Because the boat was, indeed, packed to the gunnels again.

All the predictions of a 5–7 season (the bloggers were conceding wins over Northwestern and Indiana but no one else) were forgotten. All the forecasts of a bid for the Motor City Bowl, played in Detroit and administered—ahh, the horror—by former MSU biggies, were scratched off the card. The gloom has dissipated like an October morning fog, and the autumn trees were beautiful again.

Okay. Maybe there needs to be a recalibration.

Maybe there won't be a third straight Rose Bowl trip. Not with two losses, and besides, that was unlikely from the start because Pasadena is the site of the BCS championship game in January. But there are still bowl dates to keep in Miami or Tempe, or at this season's Atlanta version of the Sugar Bowl. Even Orlando and Tampa are looking good when compared to the sourness of a week ago.

And all because of a missed field goal in overtime in East Lansing. The boat is full. The fair-weather brigade has returned. Loyalty has taken root once more.

But people like Matt Birnholtz never had a doubt.

"Michigan fans are the most loyal fans in the world," he stoutly declares. He also knows that the first game Michigan ever played was a 1–0 victory over Racine in 1879 and that Tom Harmon was the greatest Wolverine of them all.

His knowledge is quite impressive, considering that no one has heard much from Racine's football team in the last 126 years and that Birnholtz is just 12 years old—a bit too young to have seen Old 98 take the field.

But they start 'em young at Michigan. Parents pass on an adoration of Wolverines football to their offspring much as they would religious instruction.

The analogy, in fact, is not so far-fetched. It's bred in the blood, an inexhaustible, self-renewing source of future ticket buyers and donors. There is a passionate kiddie brigade, junior-grade zealots who have heard the trumpet that never cries retreat. To their ears it sounds very much like "The Victors."

Like Bob Honchar crossing himself before the kickoff of the Northern Illinois game, it comes close to a religious experience. Like the painted M that was sunbaked into Mike Ben's chest, it stamps their childhoods.

And they would never dream of deserting the ship. Only a rat would do such a thing.

Ask Sammy Grossman about that. A junior in Ann Arbor in 2005, he has never had any question about where he would go to college. His parents are Michigan grads, as are all his uncles and aunts. He was a pretty decent high school shortstop, but a little too small to play Big Ten baseball.

Although he sent out scholarship inquiries to other schools, it was a half-hearted effort. It was apparent that he would rather watch from the sideline at Michigan than make the starting lineup anyplace else.

He was once even the poster boy for Michigan fans on a Michigan State website.

"I went up to East Lansing for that game when they screwed us by adding an extra second to the clock," he says over brunch in his Ann Arbor apartment. "It was so outrageous, I just sat there with my head in my hands after they scored the touchdown to beat us.

"I didn't know it, but somebody took my picture, and it showed up on an MSU website as part of a takeoff on those ads for MasterCard. 'Tickets to the Spartan-Michigan game: $100. Buying an MSU T-shirt to remember the win: $25. Seeing a Michigan fan in despair: priceless.' And there was my picture."

Whoever the MSU photographer was, he couldn't have picked a better subject. Grossman does take it to heart.

"I was even born in Ann Arbor," he says.

"Well, technically it was Ypsilanti," corrects his dad, David Grossman, M.D. "But when I was going to med school in Ann Arbor, we had an apartment about three blocks from Michigan Stadium. He went to his first game when he was three years old. He was practically running, he was so excited. Then he never moved from my lap the entire game. He just sat there, taking in everything that was going on.

"A year or so later it was pouring down rain one Saturday and I offered to rent a movie from Blockbuster, his choice, if he wanted to pass up the game. Sam just looked at me as if I'd gone crazy."

When Grossman was about 11 his uncle took him to an Ohio State game. They were seated behind a group of Buckeyes fans who were loudly extolling the merits of their star running back, Eddie George, and what he was going to do to the underdog Michigan team.

Instead, it was Michigan tailback Tim Biakabutuka who trampled the Buckeyes in an upset win. And as the OSU fans got quieter and quieter, Grossman got louder and louder.

"Yeah, the great Eddie George," he would yell at them. "How do you like him now? Not so good right now, right?"

Grossman refused to let up, and his uncle shrank into his coat, fearing impending disaster. But the Buckeyes fans simply sat there and took it.

"They turned around once and saw that I was just a kid," says Grossman. "What were they going to do to me? Besides, there were 100,000 Michigan fans there and not too many of them [OSU fans]. But I think next year I would like to drive down to Columbus to see a game there."

"No, you wouldn't," said his father. "Knowing you, that might not be such a good idea."

Grossman's apartment looks like any dwelling inhabited by college-age males, which is like the aftermath of a catastrophic, seismic event that somehow involved food.

Grossman's roommates, Adam Schuvall and Adam Garfinkle, are also seated around the table. A TV set is tuned to ESPN's *College Game Day*. You get the feeling the set is always tuned to ESPN.

"That's not true," says Schuvall. "During the baseball playoffs it's tuned to FOX."

Loyalty, however, is the topic of the day.

Two views of The Big House, Michigan Stadium. The top image was taken in 1995 and the bottom one in 1998, after seating was added to the already 100,000-plus-capacity stadium.

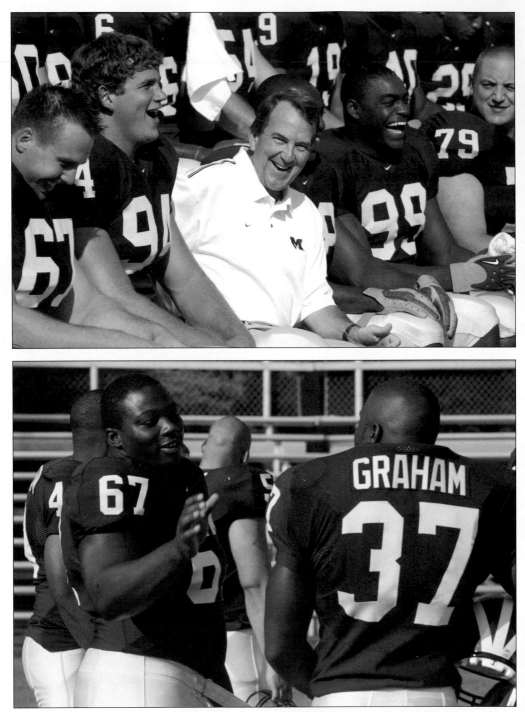

The team prepares for the start of the season at Media Day in Ann Arbor on August 8, 2005. Above, Head Coach Lloyd Carr laughs with a group of players during a photo session while, below, defensive tackle Terrance Taylor (No. 67) chats it up with linebacker Chris Graham during a break in the action.

Michigan fans get into the spirit of the season with a chance to meet the players (top) at Fan Day on August 27 and at a pep rally (below) on Friday, September 9, the day before the Wolverines were to meet Notre Dame.

Coach Carr ponders a move on the sideline during the Minnesota game at Michigan Stadium on October 8.

Wide receiver Mario Manningham celebrates his game-winning touchdown catch, sealing Michigan's 27–25 victory over Penn State on October 15 in Ann Arbor.

Michigan players Charles Stewart (No. 5), Eugene Germany (No. 96), and Kyle Myers (No. 53) celebrate the Penn State win with fans in the stands.

Coach Carr and the Wolverines prepare to take the field at Michigan Stadium to do battle with Ohio State on November 19.

Mike Massey (left) jumps onto Tyler Ecker to celebrate Ecker's touchdown in the Alamo Bowl against Nebraska on December 28 in San Antonio.

Michigan's 2005 season ended on one of the most incredible plays in recent memory, a last-gasp, seven-lateral adventure that took them from their own 36-yard line all the way to Nebraska's 13 before Ecker was finally knocked out of bounds as time expired, allowing the Huskers to survive a 32–28 Alamo Bowl thriller.

"I agree that Michigan fans are the most loyal," says Grossman.

"How can you say that?" asks one of the Adams. "The week before the State game you were saying they were going to lose all the rest of their games and that they needed to fire all their coaches."

"That was just my way of coping," says Grossman, which apparently settles things.

"To tell you the truth, I was pulling for Michigan to beat State extra hard this year," says Grossman's mother, Donna. "Two days later was the start of the Jewish holidays. If Michigan had lost, I knew Sammy would have sat at the dinner table and refused to eat. I heaved a big sigh of relief when that field goal went through."

"The only people who were really giving up," says Grossman, "were the East Coast girls. They're all spoiled."

"Now wait a minute," says Shuvall, who grew up on Long Island and lives in New Jersey. "That's not fair. Lots of girls from Michigan were giving up, too."

Shuvall, like many students from the East Coast, chose Michigan because of its aura of big-time sports. "For me it came down to a choice between Cornell and Michigan," he says. "I came to a football game here and fell in love with the place.

"ESPN took a poll on which school has the top football and basketball programs combined. Usually, it's one or the other. Michigan came in first."

"I'd have picked Texas," says Finkelstein.

Sam turns to him and snorts.

"Texas," he repeats derisively.

It is a day for loyalty.

Among some of the older Michigan fans, however, there are those who are starting to wonder whether this loyalty thing is supposed to be a two-way street. Because in recent years the athletics department has put the screws to them.

Many of them have owned season tickets since the 1960s, when they were something less than a hot commodity. They have renewed every year since—out of loyalty, they claim. Some of them, eventually, chose to improve their seat location by becoming members of the Victors, an organization for the bigger donors to the department. This move swept them out of the end zone and into seats between the 20-yard lines.

Up until the 1980s, the required gift was only $10,000, and you could make the donation in the form of a life insurance policy, with the university as the beneficiary. But that practice ended as the demand for seats went up. You had to cough up hard cash, although donors were given a few years to come up with the necessary amount.

When they first became Victors, the fans were told that this donation was a one-time gift. The university would not come back to them and tack a surcharge onto their seats.

You know how that goes, though. Things change. In 2004 all seat holders outside the end zone were told that they would have to pay an annual license fee to hold on to their prime accommodations.

According to these donors (none of whom wanted to be quoted by name, interestingly enough), the athletics department admitted that it had, indeed, made the promise not to come back for more. But it also pleaded mitigating circumstances.

It argued that almost every other school in the Big Ten has gone to a seat license arrangement. Funding for the athletics department also is handled separately from the rest of the university budget. Donations to the athletics department are not especially high on a per capita basis, either, when measured against gifts to other universities in the conference.

So the seat licenses were a financial necessity.

For seats between the 40s, the license would cost $500 per seat per year. The scale then graduated downward to $175 per seat for seats between the 20s and the end zones. That was on top of the standard ticket charge, which in 2005 was about $400 per seat.

There was a good deal of grumbling about this; actually there was a great deal of grumbling because many of the seat holders were attorneys, for whom we all know grumbling is second nature. But because there was never a written contract governing fees for these seats, the grumblers quickly realized that grumbling was all they could do.

The university also tossed a sop their way. In recent years there had been a good deal of angst about transferring seats as part of an inheritance. A lot of Old Blues wanted their family members to keep the seats long after they had shuffled off to The Big House in the sky. But the university was becoming adamant in opposing such bequests, arguing that they would block new applicants from ever obtaining seats.

So along with the seat license fee came the chance to transfer seats to younger family members. It would be a one-time offer. And, oh yes, the fee for that would be $500 per ticket.

More than 95 percent of these ticket holders bit the bullet and renewed. They were, after all, fairly affluent individuals to begin with, and a portion of the charge was also tax deductible.

The end-zone ticket holders escaped these add-on charges. But the university had a little something extra for them, too.

Many of them were a part of groups that had bought seats together for years. Their children had grown up watching Michigan football together. But now they were informed that they could buy these tickets only in blocks of eight. If they wanted guaranteed seating together for groups bigger than that, the annual cost would be $500 per ticket.

So for one group of 50 people, it meant an additional $21,000. Pay up or be scattered to the winds of chance. Most paid.

Among the Victors it was regarded as a matter of course that if you wanted priority for seats to big road games or to a bowl, you had to make an additional contribution—maybe $1,000 per year.

But even that has changed. When one longtime member put in what he thought was a routine request for seats at Ohio State, he was told that his giving level no longer was sufficient. Those seats would go to bigger fish.

So a fairly hefty portion of the Michigan fan base has come away with the idea that they are being worked over; if they didn't like it, well, there were plenty more out there who would be delighted to pay the price for their tickets.

They paid the price. But in return they expect a program that will continue to be dominant.

When you go to buy someone's loyalty, chances are he won't stay bought.

It all works out just as long as Michigan wins. If not, better watch out.

October 8:
Minnesota 23,
Michigan 20

They file out of The Big House with the look of people who have just been informed that their father is a Mafia bagman.

Stunned doesn't even begin to describe it. It is more like electrocuted.

Just as sickly as the silence that descended upon Spartan Stadium a week ago is the suffocating miasma that now has fallen upon Ann Arbor.

The Wolverines failed again, and the season has taken a desperate turn. The apparent revival of the previous week was only an illusion.

This is the team that blundered to defeat at Wisconsin, not the unit that stood up to everything that State had to throw at them and reduced Coach Carr to tears of gratitude.

The Little Brown Jug is not the rivalry it used to be. It dates back to 1903, the first game in the long series, when the Michigan players didn't trust the Gophers to supply drinkable water and brought their own container to Minneapolis to ensure a fresh supply. That game ended in a 6–6 tie, regarded as an upset for Minnesota, and in the postgame celebration, Michigan forgot the jug. When they met again, six years later, Minnesota suggested they play for the jug. And so it has gone.

When Minnesota ruled college football, in the 1930s and early 1940s, they beat Michigan nine straight times. Even Harmon, "Old 98" himself, couldn't wrest it away from the Gophers. In the last four decades, though, Minnesota has been just another also-ran, invited into The Big House for an inevitable thumping. In their last 16 meetings, since the last time Minnesota won in 1986, Michigan has run up an average of 39 points per game on them.

True, they've been getting closer. It took an incredible comeback to beat the Gophers at Minneapolis in 2003, and Michigan had to eke out a three-point win at home last year. Still, the last time Michigan lost to both Wisconsin and Minnesota in the same season was 1962.

So it is easy to see why numbness was the order of the day here. Because this just can't be happening. Even the patsies are slapping the Wolverines around.

It wasn't even the loss so much as it was the way the loss occurred.

Henne was all over the place again and couldn't move the team at all in the second half. Two critical third-down passes were thrown to tight end Massaquoi—who is playing with a cast on his hand, for God's sake.

The quarterback missed wide receivers running wide-open in the Minnesota secondary. When the Gophers moved eight men into the box to stop the running of Mike Hart, the passing game failed to loosen them up. The two Minnesota tailbacks repeatedly ripped through the Michigan defense, though, both of them finishing with over 100 yards rushing.

Michigan failed to put pressure on Minnesota's quarterback the way it had on Stanton at State. On the other hand, Henne was rushed repeatedly. And Rivas missed two field goals, one a dead-center shot in the fourth quarter from the 24-yard line.

Still, with one minute to play, it was 20–20. Minnesota's quarterback had finally been sacked and was out of the game with an injury. It was third-and-a-lot, deep in Gophers territory, and most of the crowd was already conceding another overtime to sweat out.

Then tailback Gary Russell got the ball, bounced to the outside, and, incredibly, was running free down the sideline. Everyone in the stadium knew a run was coming, a run that was designed simply to eat up as many seconds as possible so the clock would run out on regulation. But Michigan failed to contain. Russell was finally brought down inside the Michigan 20. Two plays later, Minnesota kicked the winning field goal.

Just like that, it's now a 3–3 year.

After the Wisconsin loss, the fans were predicting a 5–7 season. They didn't really mean it, though. Like Sammy Grossman, it was merely their way of coping with a disappointing start that surely would be righted.

But now that outcome was looming as a definite possibility. Because if you can't beat either Wisconsin or Minnesota, who can you beat?

Worse yet, when cornerback Leon Hall was interviewed on Monday, he said that some of his teammates were "loafing" on Russell's big run, not moving as quickly or decisively as they should have to cut off his running lane.

This is simply not done in the Michigan football program. You do not criticize. You do not antagonize. You are taught to expect nothing and do something. Accusations like this one are handled internally and, if true, will be taken care of privately by the coaches.

Moreover, Hall had been personally chosen to face the media by Carr, who is notoriously stingy about granting access to his players.

After realizing what he had said, Hall went in and apologized to his coach, who described his statement as "part of the growing process." But the damage had been done. Another fracture had appeared in this supposedly model program.

The Minnesota players raced across the field to grab the Jug, the oldest trophy in college sports.

For Michigan, the Jug has receded in importance, far behind the games with State and Ohio State. But the Minnesota players rushed to take it and then jubilantly tried to plant their banner at the 50-yard line. Michigan fans watched in silent disgust at such unseemly behavior. That's what State did when it beat Notre Dame this year. Michigan teams don't act that way. They expect to win.

Only not this year.

Later in the day, Penn State defeated Ohio State, 17–10. The fans at Happy Valley waved huge signs that read: "We're back."

For Michigan, it was a reminder of mortality. There was a time when Penn State's football program had seemed as impervious to failure as Michigan's. Under Joe Paterno, the Nittany Lions won two national titles and, in their first year in the Big Ten, had stormed undefeated through the conference and into the Rose Bowl. Some believe they were cheated out of a third national title that year.

When they entered the Big Ten it was understood that Penn State would join Michigan and OSU as perennial powers, always a threat for the title. But in only one year since 2000 has Penn State finished with a winning record.

If it could happen to them...

"We're back," said the sign. Was that a glimpse of the future in Ann Arbor?

And Joe Pa is coming in undefeated next weekend.

Thursday, October 13

WJR-AM announces that it is switching back to carrying Michigan State football as of next season. This announcement is greeted among Michigan fans as if a treacherously planted grenade has gone off at the Union.

Station president Mike Fezzey says it is a "purely business decision." And, in truth, there has been a lot of station-switching among local teams in recent years. The main Detroit outlet for the Lions, for example, is now an FM station, and the Tigers switched from WJR to a station with a far weaker signal.

There was a time when a car radio in Florida could pick up WJR after sundown on a clear night. In places like North Carolina it came in like a local station. With satellite radio, that is less important these days. But it was always a touch of home for travelers or transplants, and a way to keep up intimately with the local teams.

Being on WJR was a mark of prestige. Now it's just a matter of bottom-line calculations.

So while this is something less than a seismic shift, it is a coup for Michigan State and something of a letdown for Michigan fans. Maybe even a slap. Is this another indication of the shape of things to come, a harbinger of further humiliation in this uncertain season?

The U-M athletics department seemed to be stunned by the decision, with AD Bill Martin saying that he thought negotiations were going along "in good faith." But the deal also included MSU basketball, an increasingly important draw, and other reciprocal tie-ins with State.

Beyond that is the fate of the longtime Michigan football broadcast team, Frank Beckmann and Jim Brandstatter.

Beckmann has branched out in recent years as the host of a late-morning talk show on WJR. But his base was sports. He did Tigers games for a while but lost that gig when the team switched stations. Then he did some of their TV games but lost that job when the Tigers decided to televise only on cable. He was the voice of the Lions for many years but lost that title when they, too, left WJR.

Now Michigan is leaving the station. Beckmann has been so tied to that program that it is doubtful MSU will retain him. And he is so tied to WJR that another station would find it hard to use him. He looks to be the odd man out again.

The case with Brandstatter is clearer. At State he is regarded as something of a turncoat. His brothers all played at MSU, and he attended East Lansing High. But he was a right tackle at Michigan on Schembechler's first three teams. He has become closely identified with the Wolverines and even has written books on Michigan football history.

Brandstatter kept his job as color analyst when the Lions switched stations, reportedly because of pressure brought by interested parties in the Michigan program. It is highly unlikely that he will be retained at WJR by MSU, but he could switch to another station this time, too. Michigan takes care of its own.

It's only radio. Yet something important seems to be slipping away.

In a *Coaching Legends* television show this week, Schembechler stated that he didn't believe Michigan could come out of this slide. Too many injuries. Both starting safeties went down in the Minnesota game, and the offensive line is still a patchwork. Too much inconsistency on the offense.

National network commentator Gary Danielson says that Henne faced defenses last year that were stacked to stop Braylon Edwards, and so he had a number of options on every down. But there are no game-breakers on the Michigan offense this year. At least, none have yet emerged. Defensive coordinators do not have to get out of their usual sets when they play Michigan.

So Henne is now facing "the full package," says Danielson, and "he doesn't look like a comfortable player."

Michigan last got off to a 3–3 start in 1990. It then won every game left on its schedule, including a New Year's Day bowl.

But that was then. Penn State is now.

Saturday Morning, October 15

Ben DeSantis sounds like a reasonable enough fellow on the phone.

Working for a master's degree in education at Liberty University in Lynchburg, Virginia. Twenty-five years old. Good, expressive writer. Grew up in Pennsylvania with parents who were acolytes of Joe Pa. Switched his loyalty in all sports to Michigan when he watched them win the 1989 NCAA basketball tournament on TV. The résumé of a reasonable man.

But DeSantis is a blogger, and he wants to fire Carr yesterday if not sooner. He wants to dismiss the entire staff of assistants. He wants heads to roll.

Most of all, he wants to attend a Michigan game—because he has never actually seen the Wolverines play, except on the tube.

"Going to Ann Arbor to watch Michigan play Ohio State… that would be the ultimate. That's the mecca of the sports world," he says.

He may be 600 miles from The Big House. He may never have walked through its gates. But he knows for a fact that Carr is the only thing standing in the way of more national championships for Michigan.

In this conviction he joins a growing legion of similarly far-flung commentators who want nothing more than Carr's pate on a platter.

The FireLloydCarr.us website is up and running. That isn't DeSantis's baby, but he heartily concurs in the sentiment.

The site, which features a picture of Carr yelling and pointing with a diagonal red line drawn across it—the universal symbol of negativity—is the brainchild of another distant fan. John Lynch lives in Georgia, having moved away from Michigan when he was 11.

But distance does not lend enchantment. He, too, is convinced that Michigan must emerge from the reign of Carr, much like a frog must cast off the spell of an evil sorcerer to become princely once more.

"Here's the deal," writes Lynch. "The University of Michigan will never compete year in and year out for the national championship if we don't force action to remove this coaching staff."

He wants alumni and fans to write Athletics Director Martin and demand a change to a "younger, energetic, unpredictable, inspiring coaching staff."

"Big Ten titles are great, but national championships…are legendary. … The University of Michigan has more victories than any other school. This record is in jeopardy under Carr and his coaching staff."

Lynch has thoughtfully attached a petition to his website so fans can forward these sentiments to Martin.

He deliberately modeled the site after the one that was credited with taking down Florida head coach Ron Zook during the 2004 season.

But while DeSantis likes Lynch's spunk, he doesn't know if the cases are parallel.

"Zook replaced a legend in Steve Spurrier, a guy who won a national championship at Florida," he says. "That case was more valid. I don't think Michigan fans will respond to that sort of thing. They're too steeped in tradition."

There may also be a problem with that word *unpredictable*. After 37 straight years of winning, a little predictability may not be something that Michigan fans abhor.

"But things are mounting up," says DeSantis. "All these three- and four-loss seasons. Losing the first road game every September. The way Carr can't seem to manage big games. He has the talent to stretch the field. He doesn't have to rely on beating down the opponent in the second half. That's why Michigan keeps getting upset. He lets the other team hang in the game too long instead of finishing them off fast."

DeSantis, despite having never attended a press conference or seen the man in person, describes Carr's relationship with the media as "dry as an apricot."

"The skeptics will say that Carr should get a break because he's won nearly 100 games at Michigan along with all the Big Ten titles and the 1998 [sic] national championship," he writes. "Pure rubbish. The sports world, even at the college level, has become a 'What have you done for me lately?' enterprise. ... Carr's time has come."

Bloggers in every field of endeavor have become a media force in the new century. Some would say this proves that for every technological advance there is a step backward. But along with their more verbal cousins on sports talk radio, they have made an undeniable impact.

Accountable to no one for any misinformation they may spread. Never having to personally face anyone they attack. Heavy on opinion that is unencumbered by facts. All they need is a computer and a grievance.

There are at least a dozen Michigan football blogs. Some of them obviously have access to inside information.

When Jake Long went down with his injury before the season began, for example, Carr was characteristically vague about its nature and how it happened. But within the day bloggers were describing how Long got tangled up with 331-pound nose tackle Gabe Watson in a scrimmage and had his leg rolled over. Obviously someone who witnessed it passed the information on, knowingly or not, to a blogger who had it in print before the traditional media had all the facts.

So their presence is felt. Along Greene Street this morning, on the route that the band takes to the stadium, people already are passing out the "Fire Lloyd" petitions.

In truth, Lynch and DeSantis are saying nothing more than what is being grumbled about among the loyalists in the Victors Club. They're just more open and direct about it.

Because the question hangs out there. If Michigan keeps getting recruiting classes that are consistently described as among the best in the country every year, why doesn't it win more than it does? By a simple deductive process, it has to be the coaching

A moment, please. Let us peruse the record.

Carr took over from Gary Moeller after his unfortunate meltdown in a Detroit-area restaurant before the 1995 season. Going into this year, Carr's record was 95–29.

Over the same period, Bobby Bowden was 102–22 at Florida State. Phil Fulmer was 101–25 at Tennessee. Frank Beamer was 94–30 at Virginia Tech. Bowden won one national title, playing most of that time in a weak conference. Fulmer won one national title. Beamer didn't win any. No other coaches have comparable records over Carr's tenure at Michigan.

Against nationally ranked teams he was 35–21. In games against higher-ranked opponents the record was 17–6. In his 10 seasons as Michigan's head coach, Carr is 5–5 in the season's final game. Schembechler was 6–14–1 (although for one win and one loss he was hospitalized on game day).

So what's the problem here?

Part of it is the long shadow of the man whose office remains in Schembechler Hall.

China has the Ming Dynasty, Michigan has the Bo Dynasty, and Carr is its reigning successor. It is now in its 37th year.

The entire story of Michigan football since 1901 can be summed up in the careers and lasting influence of three coaches—Fielding Yost, Fritz Crisler, and Bo Schembechler. Their tenures and those of their disciples span 105 seasons. It is this incredible continuity that is the distinguishing feature of Michigan's history, and it is also a big part of the discontent.

When the Yost era ran out of steam after 37 years with four consecutive nonwinning seasons, Michigan went outside the system to pluck Crisler from Princeton. When that regime faltered after 31 years, Schembechler was brought in from Miami of Ohio.

After this season, the Bo Dynasty will have outlasted both of the others. Even though Michigan's offensive plans, especially the philosophy toward the forward pass, have undergone a sea of change in the last 15 years, the popular perception remains that the approach of the coaching staff is still mired in the past, a prisoner of Schembechler Hall.

You hear the complaints everywhere. The Michigan schemes on both sides of the ball are too conservative, too predictable, especially inside the opponent's red zone.

It seems to be handoff to the tailback, incomplete pass in the corner of the end zone, then another handoff to set up the field goal. Why isn't there more pressure on other quarterbacks, more blitzing, more of an attacking defense?

The fans see other Big Ten teams going to the spread, lining up wideouts all over the place, passing on any and every down, lighting up the scoreboard. They want some of that action, too.

Or maybe what they want is a change, something new after 37 years. Before he went to Florida, Meyer said that Michigan was one of the coaching jobs he would leave his contract at Utah for. Now they talk about Bobby Petrino at Louisville or Bobby Johnson at Vanderbilt.

"Give them Michigan's budget and recruiting base and see what they'd do with it," pleads DeSantis.

While there is a sizable number of Michigan fans who agree with Lynch and DeSantis, they are reluctant to say so out loud. They don't want to create an image of a system in ferment, one that is on the cusp of upheaval. They fear that perception would, eventually, affect recruiting.

"I don't believe that anything I'm doing will hurt Michigan football," DeSantis says. "When I was an undergrad at North Carolina, I wrote a column for *The Daily Tar Heel* that was highly critical of the basketball program. They just won the NCAA championship, so I guess it didn't do them any harm. In fact, it may help in recruiting because it shows how much people care, how much enthusiasm there is for the program.

"Of course, there are a lot of ignorant fans who use their blogs for propaganda."

But change for the sake of change can be a dangerous thing. Just ask the Detroit Lions, who have pursued that principle without success for six decades. Or the Nebraska fans who clamored to have Frank Solich fired and then experienced their first losing season in 43 years when the new coach's system didn't fit the personnel.

Maybe the single greatest factor for this age of discontent, however, is the Bowl Championship Series. There is a good reason that coaches do not want a playoff format in college football and are not altogether thrilled with the BCS, either.

Before its advent, the winners of all the New Year's Day bowl games could all run off the field with their pointer fingers raised high. "We're number one." And if there was a dispute in the polls over who actually merited that claim, well, all the better. The more number ones the merrier, as far as the coaches were concerned.

But now, through a highly imperfect selection process involving polls, computers, goat entrails, strength of schedule rankings, and phases of the moon, two teams are selected out of all the rest and the winner is named undisputed champion of college football.

In almost every season since it was installed, this process has produced a massive failure. On two occasions, teams that couldn't even win their own conference championship were chosen for the big game. When Auburn went undefeated through a murderous Southeastern Conference schedule in 2004, it was still the odd team out of the championship game. One year Miami defeated Florida State head-to-head and finished with the same record. But because of a flaky computer program, the Seminoles played for the title and the Hurricanes played in an irrelevant bowl. Pac-10 teams are at a consistent disadvantage because their games end after many of the voters have toddled off to slumberland.

It also provides positive incentives for running up the score on a hopelessly beaten opponent to impress clueless voters in the polls.

With all its flaws, however, the BCS title game is still accepted as the goal. The Rose Bowl is no longer enough. That was the gold standard when Schembechler was coaching. You just had to finish ahead of nine other teams and you went to Pasadena. A reasonable annual pursuit. But now you have to beat out more than 100 teams in Division I-A to get into the BCS championship. Even Southern California, supposedly going for a historic three straight championships this season, didn't make it into the BCS game in 2003. The "official" winner that year was Louisiana State, while USC led the AP poll. It was exactly that sort of split decision that the BCS was created to avoid. Good job, fellas.

It is an almost impossible goal to make the BCS game every year, yet it's what the bloggers seem to expect. Even after two straight Rose Bowls, Carr is weighed in the balance and found light by several pounds.

Pasadena is passé. The glory road runs there only once every four years, and any other destination but the BCS is perceived as failure.

7

October 15:
Michigan 27,
Penn State 25

I t turns out that Joe Pa wasn't too old at 78. He was just
too late by one second.

And if the bloggers don't like Carr as a coach, they've
got to give him points as a debater.

After surrendering the apparent winning touchdown to the
Nittany Lions with less than a minute to play, Michigan began
its final desperate effort. As it turned out, the critical point
came with 28 seconds left. Carr ran on the field and began
furiously arguing with the officiating crew that Michigan's
last timeout, called from the sideline, had been granted too
slowly. He wanted four seconds put back on the clock.

The officials huddled and in their Solomonic wisdom decided to split the difference and give Carr two seconds. Although Paterno raged, it didn't seem to matter much at the time. Just two more seconds in which to suffer until the inevitable end. Because this was exactly the sort of game, say the bloggers, that Carr cannot manage.

But when a sideline pass was completed to the 10, there was still one second remaining on the clock. If Carr hadn't convinced the officials of the lapse in time, the game would have been over.

So Henne was given one final fling to Manningham, running free across the back of the end zone, and Michigan won a most improbable victory. Maybe the craziest since Anthony Carter raced down the field against Indiana after time had expired in 1979. Or maybe since the first game Carr coached at Michigan—the 18–17 defeat of Virginia in 1995 on Scott Dreisbach's end-zone pass to Mercury Hayes as time ran out.

But Carter's catch had come on a 6–1 team, and Dreisbach's little miracle was in the Pigskin Classic "preseason" game.

This most recent one may have meant even more, because it came with Michigan staring into the abyss. No, halfway down the maw.

Wisconsin and Minnesota already had beaten them in the last minute, and now it was happening again. At home. For the second straight week. No chance for a Big Ten title. A good chance at a losing season.

This can't be happening.

When the ball left Henne's hand, that one second seemed to stretch into eternity. And when Manningham gathered it in, The Big House erupted in emotional tumult.

Strangers slapped hands, fathers hugged their children, elderly women waved their arms as if suddenly recalling the steps to the Lindy.

The entire team raced into the end zone to swarm Manningham and pile, howling, onto the turf. The band was right behind them, too overwrought to even start another chorus of "The Victors."

Then the players began leaping into the student section, high-fiving the kids and exchanging bear hugs with them.

It was as if the Wolverines had just clinched another title, not merely staved off the total collapse of their season. And just like that they had found their big-play receiver.

Somewhere amid all the hilarity on the field was Mark Snyder, in his first year as the Michigan beat writer for the *Detroit Free Press.*

For someone who has never been there, it's hard to convey how insulated you are in the press box. The thick plateglass windows mute the crowd noise. Little of the passion in the stands makes it through. And, of course, the one inviolable rule is "No cheering in the press box." This is a place to work, not to root. No one up there raises a right hand on each repetition of "Hail" when they play "The Victors."

Over the years, several newspaper commentators have remarked on the lack of emotion among Michigan fans. It certainly must seem that way from where they sit.

In the era when Michigan could be counted on to steamroll everything in its path until Ohio State, it may even have been true. But these are different times. Dangerous times. This season it seems that almost any team in the conference is capable of beating Michigan, even in The Big House. And the emotional quotient has risen accordingly.

Sitting in the stands these days can even be a little discomfiting for those accustomed to the antiseptic precincts of the press. To watch middle-aged fans pleading, almost tearfully, for a 19-year-old kid to produce a miracle and preserve their dreams is wrenching.

In the Penn State section, many of the blue-and-white left the stadium right after their team's touchdown, which was scored right in front of them. They were secure in the knowledge that they had witnessed a famous victory. Their season was still perfect. Those who remained in their seats stared at the field with the same sort of sickly horror that Michigan fans had slapped across their faces the previous week.

"How you like us now?" screamed one of the elated Wolverines fans in the neighboring seats. "How you like us now?"

There's no empathy in football.

At the farthest end of the field, Snyder was scribbling notes furiously and trying to find Manningham amid the mob.

"They allow the press to stand along the sidelines in the fourth quarter," he said. "Access to the players is so limited that you almost have to go down there to try to grab someone before they get back to the locker room, because you have no control over who Lloyd will bring to the press conference after the game. That is totally up to him. If past experience was any guide, it wasn't going to be a freshman like Manningham.

"I was trying to get a feel for the emotion so I could put it in the lead of my story, trying to talk to as many players as I could. I'd already spoken a few days before to Tim Massaquoi about what this game meant to the players from Pennsylvania, guys who had been recruited by Penn State. Him and Steve Breaston and Henne. As emotional as this was for everyone else, it was even more for them. Breaston was the first one into the stands, and the others followed him."

Snyder is in a strange position for a sportswriter. Several, in fact.

Under the terms of the joint operating agreement between Detroit's two newspapers, the *Free Press* does not publish a sports page on Sunday. That means his account of Saturday's game will not appear until Monday morning, making it imperative for him to develop a story that goes beyond touchdowns and field goals. He must find a slant that will hold up for two days and is distinct from what his competitor at *The Detroit News* is writing.

In 2006 the situation will be reversed because of ownership changes at the two papers. *The News* will have no Sunday paper at all, and Snyder will be free to cover the team in a more conventional manner. But that's another story for another season.

For the 2005 season he must be content to write a first-day game story that appears only in the online edition of the paper. No one knows how many people will actually read it, but he must write it, and, for his own peace of mind, it must be good.

The other element is that he went to Michigan and grew up in a family of avid Michigan fans. He also covered the football team in his senior year at *The Michigan Daily* during the 1998 season.

"I made a commitment back then that if I was serious about being a sportswriter, I had to stop being a fan," he said.

"My family doesn't believe it. It frustrates my old friends from school. They don't really think that I'm not up there in the press box secretly cheering Michigan on, even if I can't show it.

"But it's true. For me it's just a matter of dealing with the problems that come with covering this team. Some people even ask me, 'Well, don't you really want Michigan to win because when the team does well, more people will read your story?' Not really. Michigan has such a huge following that the stories will be read no matter if the team wins or loses. It's not personal. I think it's a disservice to the reader to feel any different."

Michigan football is a major beat, one that any sportswriter would covet. As a little bonus, the job almost always involves a winter trip to a warm bowl in California or Florida. In Carr's first year as coach, the team ended up in Texas, but such an unseemly detour has never been repeated.

Still, covering this team is never a day at the beach. Carr, like Schembechler before him, believes in keeping tight controls on access to his players. The media is barred from the locker room and most practices.

"He gives what he thinks is enough," says Snyder, "but you never are able to get what you regard as the whole story."

The format seldom varies. After the game, Carr and carefully selected players will walk over to Crisler Arena, right next to the stadium, and enter the pressroom. Each player will answer some questions from the reporters, Carr will make a statement, and everyone leaves.

There is no access to players or coaches on Sunday, although many other schools, Michigan State and Notre Dame among them, allow it.

Monday is the biggest day of Snyder's work week. There is always a noon press luncheon that Carr attends along with about four players. After the Penn State game, he chose Henne; Alan Branch, a sophomore defensive end who played well; senior offensive lineman Rueben Riley; and Carl Tabb, who is listed as a wide receiver but was inserted into the game briefly as a running quarterback, the position he played in high school.

Each player answers questions from the group of reporters and then stands behind a podium for more personalized interviews.

"If you follow one player to the podium," said Snyder, "you miss what someone else is saying. So you have to plot out who you're going to talk to in advance. It's the closest we can get to a one-on-one interview, and I have to get enough material out of this day to get me through the rest of the week."

Carr then closes the meeting by answering questions about the team and Saturday's game. Reporters quickly learn that his answers are honest and direct, but limited. Questions about injuries are off-limits because Carr believes such information gives the opposition an edge.

"But if you bring up a subject that he cares about—say, the team's strength program or steroid use among athletes—he can go off on a fascinating lecture," said Snyder. "He is very well-read, and what he says is authoritative. He's also a little more open than he was when I covered him for *The Daily*."

On Tuesday there is a two-hour teleconference in which all coaches from the Big Ten appear for a few minutes. This is Snyder's chance to get some information from next week's coaching opponent.

The rest of his week is spent writing about the stuff he gathered on Monday—a question-and-answer session, a personality profile on a player, and background analysis of the upcoming game. If it's a road game, he's on a plane by Friday afternoon.

"Sure, I read the bloggers," he said. "I think that's now part of the job. I have to monitor them to make sure they didn't get information I don't have. That can happen, and the onus is on the mainstream media to make sure it doesn't. Parents, high school coaches, prominent alumni all get access to the team that we don't, and some of that information ends up on the blogs. Same thing with sports talk radio. Most of it is just people venting, but if a Gary Danielson is going to offer an analysis, I try to listen. He just has more insight into the game of football than I do."

Snyder finds his readers even more vehement in their denunciations of Carr than the bloggers. Before the Penn State game, Snyder estimated they were running 90–10 against the coach.

"The passion is incredible," he said. "I've been blown away by the standard they set for this team. The graduates, the alumni, the fans with no particular ties to the university... they feel so much more strongly about it than the students.

"And they insist I should be writing that the school fire Carr or fire Herrmann. They don't understand, first of all, that isn't the function of the beat writer. That's the sort of thing a columnist should handle. Second of all, I don't have that kind of influence. It's ridiculous that they think I do. But they have so much emotion invested in Michigan football. Which is why, I suppose, it's such a great assignment."

If you didn't get emotional over this game, it's time to get your pulse checked.

But back in Old Virginny, DeSantis described the victory as "bittersweet."

"It was great to see Michigan win, especially since it was Penn State, the school my parents root for," he said. "I expected a double-digit loss.

"On the other hand, it buys Carr more breathing room. On ESPN they were even saying that he should be coach of the week, and I was screaming at the TV set, 'Are you kidding me? They gave up more than 400 yards of total offense.'"

Bloggers are just not happy people.

Besides, next up is Iowa. The Hawkeyes haven't lost at home in the last three years, and Michigan still hasn't won two in a row this season.

Maybe this is the week Carr's breathing room will run out.

Monday, October 18

Two days after watching his favorite team upend Penn State, Michael Ben (he of the painted *M* on his bare chest) was presented with an even nicer surprise. His first child was born two weeks ahead of schedule.

She came home from the hospital wrapped in a maize-and-blue blanket. This was altogether understandable. While she was still in the womb, Ben and his wife would sometime respond to her kicking by singing "The Victors" to her. You never can start 'em too young.

"I'm not surprised about the blanket," said Bud Van De Wege Jr. "Michigan insignia gifts for infants and toddlers have become one of our biggest sellers."

Van De Wege is the owner of Moe Sport Shops, two sports apparel stores that specialize in Michigan items and are always called "Moe's." Founded in 1915, they are an Ann Arbor institution, one located across the street from the Diag. The stores have been run by the Van De Wege family for more than 40 years.

"There is a very strong emotional component to this business," said Van De Wege. "After the Minnesota game, for example, we had almost no one come in here. That game was what I called a trunk-slammer. People were so upset that all they wanted to do was throw their stuff in the car trunk, slam it shut, and go home.

"But they came the next day. It was homecoming weekend, and to many of the old grads, we're a part of the Ann Arbor they remember. We're something that hasn't changed, that's just the way it was when they were going to school here. I don't have to tell you how important tradition is at Michigan."

It was Van De Wege's father, also named Bud (actually, like his son, he's named Edwin J., but he hasn't been called that for years), who bought Moe's in 1964.

"That was a good year to get into it, a Rose Bowl year," said the elder Bud. "Michigan hadn't been to a bowl in 14 years, so there was a lot of emotion. I still hear from guys on that team. The longer you're away from a major bowl, the better business is for us. So 1964 was a very good year.

"But it didn't compare to the start of 1998, in the first days after Michigan won the national championship. We had crowds literally out the door here three days in a row. They wanted anything with "Michigan" on it. We did more business in three days than we usually do in the first three months of any year, because that is our slack season.

"It'll never be that way again, though. Almost 10 percent of our sales are over the Internet now, and there is a lot more competition."

One of the biggest competitors is Steve and Barry's, which opened up a few years ago right around the corner on State Street. This is a national chain, a 14,000-square-foot big box store, run out of the New York City area, with outlets in several college towns. The business was started up to capitalize on the growing trend for wearing and displaying college gear. Year in and year out, items bearing the Michgan name or seal come in first or second in sales.

Steve and Barry's can undercut Moe's in price, but not in tradition. And Steve and Barry's is almost as tightly controlled as Carr's team. All information requests have to be cleared first by the New York office. Some companies just seem to have the strange idea that information about a football T-shirt is somehow related to national security. Things are much more relaxed around the corner at Moe's.

"Our customers tend to come in week after week," said Bud Sr. "We now employ the children of people who worked for us when we first opened. I get a call every Monday morning from a doctor in Los Angeles who wants to talk over the last game with me. So I finally had this sweatshirt printed up and sent it to him."

He points to a photograph on a bulletin board above his desk. A smiling, gray-haired man is proudly wearing a shirt that reads, "Michigan: The crazy doctor from L.A."

Any kind of Michigan shirt imaginable is available at Moe's. Most of them are austere, dark blue with "Michigan" printed across the chest.

Some say "This is The Big House." There is also a variety of "Go Blue" shirts. There's one in French (*Allez-les-Bleus*), another in Spanish (*Vamos Azul*), and others sport Hebrew and Chinese characters.

But that only scratches the surface of Michigan paraphernalia here. Pants, socks, shoes. Golf tees and balls. Pacifiers. Drinking cups. Shot glasses. Bottle openers. Anything big enough to carry the word *Michigan* on it, or, in a pinch, just the block M.

"The breakout item is apparel specific to women," said Bud Jr. "It used to be they would just wear a unisex item in a smaller size. But women's clothing has mushroomed in this field, and it's now a dominant thing on our racks."

Moe's is also trying to go a step beyond this season, selling the pro jerseys of former Michigan stars. The floor salesman is wearing a Cleveland Browns jersey with Braylon Edwards's name on the back.

Hanging on the walls are the jerseys of Amani Toomer, Ty Law, Charles Woodson, Jon Jansen, and, of course, three-time Super Bowl winner Tom Brady.

"We'll see how it goes," said Bud Jr. "When you're a Michigan fan, it seems to carry on into their pro careers. Besides, I like the idea of having an offensive lineman like Jansen up there. That seems to be another trend in this business. Make yourself distinct by passing up the big-name star's jersey and go for someone more obscure."

Bud Sr. didn't go to Michigan. He attended Hope College in his hometown of Holland, Michigan, where he starred in basketball, then got into engineering sales on the East Coast.

"I remember sitting around with a bunch of the other guys; it was at the Lord Jeff Hotel in Amherst, Massachusetts," he said. "We were talking about what we'd like to do when we got out of sales and retired. I said that I'd like to own a sporting goods store in a college town somewhere.

"A few years after I bought this place, one of the guys who was at the Lord Jeff came into town and saw my name on the store. He walked in, shook my hand, and said, 'You son of a bitch, you did it.' I'd almost forgotten about that conversation, but I guess it really had stuck in my mind, and when the chance came to buy this store, I did it."

Bud Jr.'s sport was also basketball. He was an assistant on Bill Frieder's staff at Michigan and then took over as head coach of the women's program, where he was Big Ten Coach of the Year one season. Then he took over the family business.

Some of that business is regular and cyclical.

"After the Ohio State game we'll always have a big crowd in here," said Bud Jr. "Last game of the season and it usually means something. We even get some Columbus people who find their way in here to kid around with us.

"Hockey is good because the team is always good. But sales don't pick up until they start the Frozen Four tournament. This year it was women's softball. We never expected that. But after Michigan won the championship, people really got into it, and they wanted softball stuff."

This does not appear, however, to be a vintage football season, and the Van De Weges are braced for that.

"It looks as if the team will be going to a lesser bowl, and after two straight Rose Bowls it will mean much less of a sales impact," said Bud Sr. "But the thing about this business is that Michigan always renews itself, and you know that next year will be good again.

"It's a great life for someone who never felt much like working. It's been nothing but fun."

If you had set out to design the perfect picture of college life, it would probably resemble Ann Arbor in autumn.

In mid-October, especially, when the color is at its vibrant peak and every residential street is sheltered by a canopy of red and gold (or maize, as it is referred to here), the portrait is complete.

The light jackets come out in the morning chill, and students can see their breath as they walk to class. But by afternoon the sun has warmed the Diag to a shirtsleeve scene.

When former students recall the brightest of their college days, it is probably a day in October that they remember—when they were still too young to realize what a gift life is on days such as these.

But this year summer has overstayed its allotted time on the calendar. Like guests who have enjoyed a fine restaurant meal and refuse to give up their table to the next waiting party, the warm season has lingered on.

Terrible hurricanes have swept the South, rain has pummeled New England, and the stifling Santa Ana wind has spread fires through the canyons and hillsides of California. But in Michigan, few can remember a finer fall. It isn't even really Indian summer, because there has yet to be a frost. The October home games with Minnesota and Penn State were played in late summer weather, watched by crowds who had left their coats in their cars.

Now in the month's last 10 days, the color has finally burst forth. But the team is gone. Next up is a road game in Iowa, another at Northwestern, then a bye week before the stadium gates open again.

It seems wrong somehow. Here if ever is perfect football weather. But when the last two home games of this strange season are played, with Indiana and Ohio State, we will be in the grip of dank November. And by that time the mood at The Big House may be as empty as the trees and dark as the skies, because no one yet seems to know where this season is headed. As exhilarating as the Penn State game was, everyone also remembers how good the team looked against State; and wasn't that followed by the terrible crash against Minnesota?

Up and down, a win and a loss. No consistency anywhere.

Manningham has emerged, at last, as the big-play receiver. Breaston has recovered his former zip. Hart has restored legitimacy to a running game that had disappeared behind a makeshift offensive line. Avant is the most dependable third-down receiver in the conference. There are reports that even Jake Long may be coming back at tackle for the Iowa game. Still, an indefinable something seems to be missing.

Meanwhile, the much-maligned defense has kept the record respectable—if that is the right word for a 4–3 mark with two tough road games at hand. It's all looking good, except for that discomfiting inability to get off the field late in the fourth quarter when the game is on the line.

On the other hand, if the offense were playing with a fraction of the efficiency expected of it, those games would have been out of reach by the fourth quarter.

The Penn State game muted the critics—it didn't silence them. They still foresee, at best, a 6–5 season and a trip to the Embarrassment Bowl.

The team may be absent, but one gate remains open on the north side of the stadium. A few tourists have lined up to take each other's pictures before the Big M sculpture, with The Big House as the backdrop. It is a must stop on any collegiate sports tour, much like those destinations for baseball enthusiasts who keep a record of all the ballparks they visit.

Later the visitors may even walk into Schembechler Hall, over on State Street, and explore the Michigan museum. The cases display old footballs and trophies and photographs and sweaters that make the great tradition palpable.

You look at the faces from those teams of a century and more ago. Here is William Cunningham, Michigan's first All-American selection as a center, in 1898, hand on hip in his bulky "M" sweater. Willie Heston, the great running back from the national champions of Yost's earliest years, looking so small. Harry Kipke, captain of the 1922 team and coach of two national champions in the 1930s.

You wonder if they could possibly have understood what they were starting so many years ago. Your mind goes back to the scene in the film *Dead Poets Society*, when the teacher played by Robin Williams takes his students to the school's trophy case and talks about the long-departed faces who were once as young as they are now.

"Carpe diem," he whispers to them. "Seize the day."

Carr leads his players, especially the freshmen, in a chorus of "The Victors" before their first summer practice every year. Does he also take his players down here before the season to show them these displays? Would he, too, tell them to seize the day?

Tradition can be a light to be followed as well as a burden to be borne.

8

October 22:
Michigan 23, Iowa 20

Something significant may have happened here, but, like the sighting of a UFO, no one is quite sure what it was.

The sportswriters are using words like *heart* and *gut check* and *grittiness* to describe this team. These are not words usually associated with Michigan football. Let's face it: they are usually not the sort of qualities required to win games there. Lesser schools must scramble for respect while Michigan is the conquering hero.

In this strange season, however, it is Michigan that must resort to things like mental toughness and pride to pull out games. Talent alone isn't getting it done anymore.

But maybe that's not right, either. After all, when the fourth tailback on the depth chart scores the winning touchdown, that's still some kind of talent stockpile.

The only thing certain is that whatever is going on here, Michigan fans can't take much more of it. For the fifth game in a row, the outcome wasn't decided until the game's final minute...or beyond. Never in the recorded annals of Michigan football has there been a run like this.

Athletics department statisticians began keeping track of games decided in the fourth quarter in 1949. The closest comparison to this season was 1967, that year of evil omen, when six games saw the winning points come in the final quarter. On four such occasions those points were not scored by Michigan. But in only one of those games did the denouement actually occur within the final minute.

In 1986 two games—a win over Iowa and a loss to Minnesota—came down to a field goal as time expired. And in 1994 the Wolverines beat Notre Dame with two seconds left, then lost the next week on Kordell Stewart's heave into the end zone after time seemed to have run out for Colorado.

But never, ever were there five such games in a row—with two of them going into overtime. The heart can only stand so much.

Hart's ankle could not stand very much at all. The star running back went down in the first quarter, so the running attack stalled again. The team's best defensive player, LaMarr Woodley, got in for only two plays after suffering a deep arm bruise in practice. By the fourth quarter, Michigan was down to its fourth tailback, Jerome Jackson, and its two freshmen safeties were under fire from Iowa's Drew Tate.

Yet the Wolverines clung to a three-point lead. Henne, once more struggling for consistency, hit Breaston on a 52-yard pass that Breaston ran down the sideline midway through the quarter, making the score 17–14.

Then Iowa started moving downfield against the exhausted defense, and the familiar sinking feeling in the abdominal cavity could be felt down to one's shoes. Once again, Michigan couldn't get the big stop with the game on the line.

But Hawkeyes coach Kirk Ferentz did what all the angry bloggers and radio screamers had been accusing Carr of— when the game was up for grabs, he played not to lose.

Instead of going for the kill, once Iowa entered the red zone Ferentz turned cautious and played to set up a 32-yard field goal and get the tie. With his first crack at the ball in overtime, the calls resulted in Iowa kicking another three-pointer.

It was the same sort of conservative streak that Smith had uncharacteristically revealed in the State game. It ended up costing Ferentz in the same way.

On Michigan's overtime possession, Avant managed to twist his body around to grab a Henne pass thrown behind him at the 5. Then Jackson got it across on three carries. Carr said later that he had no intention of kicking. It was to be win or lose on that series of downs.

When Jackson scored the winner, it was right behind a block by Long, playing his first game of the season.

It was also the first time the team had won two in a row this year, and the first time Iowa had trailed on its home field in its last 11 games. On top of that it was Carr's 100th win with Michigan. He was given the game ball, and, for the second time this season, he got misty-eyed in the locker room.

He has seen this Michigan team with a foot on its windpipe almost every week. But when it is given the chance to catch its breath, it is still a dangerous outfit.

Or maybe it's more like gritty, gutsy. A team with heart.

Such strange words in a strange season.

Monday, October 24

The hounds have turned on John L. Smith. You think Carr has it tough? This guy was the man of the age in East Lansing just three weeks ago. Now they're ready to run him out of town.

The gut-wrenching loss to Michigan was followed by an equally unnerving defeat at Ohio State. When the coaches couldn't get the right players on the field for a field-goal try at the end of the second half, the kick was blocked by the Buckeyes and they ran it back for a game-breaking touchdown.

One week later Northwestern came into town and simply blew the Spartans away, 49–14. Three losses in a row and another season gone to hell for MSU.

All Smith's off-the-wall personality quirks—climbing mountains in Kenya in the off-season, slapping players across the face for good performances, a risk-taking offense—are now dismissed as negatives. Instead of the anti-Carr, he is now regarded as the anti-Christ.

Several hundred miles to the south, Tennessee fell to unbeaten Alabama 6–3 this weekend, and they are howling for Phil Fulmer's scalp. He won the national title in 1998, the year after Carr did it. The two coaches' records are remarkably similar. Fulmer's stadium is only a few dozen seats smaller than The Big House, and his teams also keep it filled.

But the Fire Fulmer websites are up and running. They are posted by fans who are far nastier than the Fire Carr forces. One of them even repeated, and then piously denied, a rumor that Fulmer would be forced to resign because he had sex with a young secretary in the athletics department offices.

"His time is past," wrote one blogger, and another indelicately referred to him as a "lard ass" who will "disgrace the great traditions of Volunteer football."

Here's a guy who brought Tennessee its first national title in almost half a century and he's going to "disgrace" its traditions? Looks like nutso time at Rocky Top.

Young males with the emotional stability of eight-year-olds are now pseudonymous lightning rods of discontent. They got Frank Solich out at Nebraska, Ron Zook at Florida. Having proven their power, they now appear to be after anyone who doesn't give them instant gratification. It's as if *Sesame Street* has come to college football.

It gets even nuttier at the Air Force Academy, where longtime coach Fisher DeBerry is not only losing but also offending the race police.

DeBerry made the comment that he needs to recruit more black athletes because they can run faster. There's a shocking piece of news all right.

If you look over the roster of every major football school, as well as the NFL, there doesn't seem to be much argument about that. The speed positions—running backs, cornerbacks, wide receivers—are almost unanimously held by African

Americans. There hasn't been a white tailback starting at Michigan, for example, since Rob Lytle in the mid-1970s.

Who knows what the reasons are. Some of them may be physiological, some may be cultural. But Fisher's statements are anathema to the politically correct, who insist that any differences between races and genders are mere perceptions and artificially imposed.

You are not permitted to say what is patently obvious if it is deemed to be offensive or, worse yet, makes people uncomfortable. At many universities, this is part of the speech code.

Paul Hornung lost a radio gig at Notre Dame for saying much the same thing a few years ago, suggesting that the school lower its admissions standards for black athletes in order to recruit superior talent. That happens all the time on the academic side, where it is called affirmative action. But again, you are not allowed to point that out.

To be fair, DeBerry is probably getting caught in the wash of earlier scandals involving sexual and religious harassment at the Academy. Still, he deserves some slack. He has won 161 games during 21 years in Colorado Springs going into the 2005 season, a remarkable record for a service academy team where entrance requirements are severe. But even the longtimers can't dodge the PC bullets.

It seems that success in the past can work against a coach because it translates into higher expectations and less patience.

Even MSU's Tom Izzo, who runs one of the most successful college basketball programs in the nation (four Final Fours and one championship), told the *Free Press* this week that the pressure of meeting the expectations he has created is almost unbearable.

It is the eternal conundrum of big-time sports. The more you win, the more winning is expected. And when you start to lose, you're just another bum. In the words of the show tune: "What did I have I don't have now?"

Michigan will be a three-point favorite against North-western. There are some who thought they should be underdogs—the first time that would have happened since Ara Parseghian coached the Wildcats in the late 1950s.

The last time Michigan lost to Minnesota, Wisconsin, and Northwestern all in the same season was 1934. You could also throw in Michigan State, Ohio State, Illinois, and Chicago. That was a 1–7 year, the worst in Michigan history, when the team scored a grand total of 21 points.

But this season, something seems to have clicked. A win at Northwestern will make the team bowl-eligible, and the specter of a losing season will finally be put to rest—at least for this year.

Tuesday, October 25

Gene Rontal, M.D., is haunted by a memory. The Detroit-area physician already has seen what can happen to a coach who comes under unbearable pressure, and he gets furious as he sees it building on Carr.

Without justification, in his view.

"It makes me angry," he says. "This team has been hit with one critical injury after another, and he's still got them right in the race. In my mind, it's the most brilliant year he's ever had as a coach.

"I can't understand the people who want to fire him. Did he fumble at the goal line against Notre Dame? Did he miss the field goal against Minnesota? He put his team in position to win both times. That's all a coach can do. The rest is on the shoulders of the players."

Rontal studied sports medicine as an undergrad at Ann Arbor. He played rugby there for George Mans, who was also an assistant coach under Schembechler. So he managed to develop a close relationship with the football program and was on the sideline for most games.

"I went up to Minnesota for my residency," he says, "and I asked Bo if I could do some scouting for him while I was there. He was probably just humoring me, but he said that would be fine. So I went to see this lineman play at a small Catholic school up there and recommended him to Bo.

"His name was Jeff Perlinger. He ended up starting at defensive tackle for two years and being named All–Big Ten. After that, Bo figured I knew what I was doing, and I did some recruiting for him when I moved back to Michigan. Of course, the NCAA has changed the rules about alumni recruiting since then, but I made trips with Larry Smith and Bill McCartney and Gary Moeller back in the 1970s.

"They all went on to be successful head coaches, and when Moeller took over for Bo in 1990, we were good friends. That's when I saw what that pressure can do to a strong person.

"I had a talk with Mo in the spring of 1995, and I could see he was just eating himself up over the previous season. The team had lost four games, including that last-second thing against Colorado and another one late to Penn State at home. He just kept talking about it.

"I told myself that I should go to someone in the program and tell them that Mo needs to take it easy. But I never did. And two weeks later he lost it at that restaurant in Southfield [Excalibur, where Moeller became publicly intoxicated], just blew wide open.

"I've regretted it ever since. So when Lloyd was named coach that year, I told myself that it wasn't going to happen again."

Rontal rounded up some prominent former Michigan athletes, including Terry Barr, Tom Maentz, and Roger Zatkoff, and sat down with Carr.

"We met at a hotel in Novi, and we never spoke about football," says Rontal. "We talked about the media and public relations and handling the pressures and expectations.

"Lloyd told me years later that it was a seminal moment for him. It gave him the perspective he needed to get through. Because those first couple of years weren't easy."

Carr won his first five games as head coach in 1995 and then went 4–4. The next season, Michigan won the first seven out of eight and then went 1–3—although a big upset over Ohio State in Columbus helped ease the sting.

Then came 1997 and the national title.

Carr had heard the discontent building during his first two years. After the second season he said, "The critical part is to be able to separate honest, intelligent criticism from all the other stuff. If you can't do that, it can get to you."

Now, nine years later, it is starting all over again.

"Bo never let the media set the agenda," says Rontal. "If anything, he intimidated the media. But that was Bo.

"Lloyd does a good job of insulating himself from the bad stuff. Once in a while he'll call and wants to know what the pulse is. But, you know, he's in Ann Arbor and the major media outlets are in Detroit, and that distance allows him some space to remove himself.

"Never underestimate the competitiveness of this guy. I've played golf with him, and he's intense as they come. He gives me pep talks when we're teamed up. 'Come on, we've got to make this shot.' I saw him hit out of a bunker 150 feet from the hole and drop it three feet from the pin. It's in his juices.

"But he's such a decent man, and that's what bothers me about this Fire Lloyd garbage. I understand the passion, the disappointment. Football as a surrogate for a lot of anger. But this is a man who is good for college football and good for the university.

"I've seen him do so many thoughtful things. I mean he actually called a play that a 90-year-old acquaintance of mine suggested and then wrote him a note saying that it wasn't called 'Old 98' anymore. The new term was 'Gator.' He didn't have to do that. This wasn't some big shooter. It was just a nice old guy, and Lloyd made him feel like a million dollars.

"I know it's football and everybody thinks he's an expert. Still, the man won a national championship. You'd think that gives him a lifetime pass."

Rontal's right about that. Still, Dan Devine resigned as coach at Notre Dame under heavy personal criticism three years after winning the title in 1977. Also at Notre Dame, Lou Holtz made a similar decision a decade and a half later. Danny Ford left Clemson as a recruiting scandal was about to blow up in his face, and Woody Hayes had to retire when he punched one of Ford's players during a bowl game.

But lifetime passes seem to expire a lot quicker these days.

October 29:
Michigan 33,
Northwestern 17

The journey gets stranger with every passing week.

If you'll recall, Michigan won its opener against Northern Illinois almost two months ago by the score of 33–17.

There were sounds of distress. The Huskies rolled up 411 yards of total offense against Michigan, which only confirmed in the minds of many that the Wolverines defense would be the undoing of this season.

How could a MAC team move the ball so easily against them? No good could come of it.

Now the very same people are lauding the very same defense for holding Northwestern to 415 yards of total offense and beating them by the very same score.

Oddly enough, when Northwestern played Northern Illinois this season, the difference was one point, 38–37. Come to think of it, maybe it wasn't all that odd.

This was a Northwestern team that had just come off an outright annihilation of MSU in East Lansing the previous week. Penn State had beaten them only in the last desperate minute in an earlier game at Evanston.

The student body, whose enthusiasm for its football team usually resembles a zombie jamboree, was geeked. There were even purple-and-white body-paint jobs in the stands. This type of behavior is usually regarded as unseemly at Northwestern—an institution whose students eagerly anticipate becoming masters of the universe.

It was also a night game. It is conventional wisdom in sports that any contest throwing an athlete's body clock awry is dangerous. Ohio State came into Evanston at night last season, for example, and was beaten.

But this Michigan season, which had the stink of despair upon it from the second week, appears to have inexplicably righted itself.

The team has won three in a row and has gone from "Will they even be bowl-eligible this year?" to "Hey, we've got a shot at a BCS bowl!"

And it is the defense that did it. Their transformation from being the baggage that the rest of the team had to overcome to becoming the backbone of the team was never more apparent than in this game.

The Wildcats came in with an offense that had to be outscored because it couldn't be contained. They had run amok against the conference's top defense in Penn State and rang up 51 on Wisconsin. No lead was safe against them.

So even when Michigan took a fast 14–0 lead, everyone understood that it wasn't going to be nearly enough. After all, Northwestern had been driving on its first possession when Leon Hall scooped up a fumble and ran 83 yards for the second Michigan touchdown.

Far from being disheartened, Brian Basanez took the ball and within 37 seconds had fired a long touchdown pass to Mark Philmore. A quick field goal closed it to 14–10, and the race to 50 seemed to be on.

Even when Michigan scored the next 13 points, including a Henne scoring pass, there didn't seem to be any way to hold off the relentless Wildcats attack. Basanez and Philmore struck again with 11 seconds left in the half, leaving Michigan with only a 10-point lead, 27–17, at the intermission.

But that was it. For the entire second half, Michigan held them scoreless. Basanez threw the ball all over the lot, but Northwestern never mounted any kind of running threat— and that was the key. With just 89 yards on the ground, the Wildcats had to pass, and Michigan was ready for a one-dimensional offense.

Basanez, who had thrown just one pick all season, was intercepted twice, chased around all evening, and unable to sustain anything.

Meanwhile, for the second straight week, Jackson emerged from the cellar of the depth chart, running for 105 yards and allowing Michigan to keep the Northwestern offense off the field for long stretches.

Henne still appeared unsure, and Rivas had to kick four short field goals, three of them from the red zone, when the Michigan offense stalled against the weakest defense in the conference.

Still, this is now a confident 6–3 team, heading into a bye week and then a game with Indiana, which many smart-asses say is like having another bye week.

No one mentions firing Herrmann anymore, either.

There are all kinds of theories about what happened to this team, what caused the transformation from the confused and outrun defenders of 2004.

The linebackers are faster. Shawn Crable, a sophomore out of the football factory in Massillon, Ohio, was on top of Basanez consistently in this game, and junior David Harris has been coming on strong all year.

The young safeties, Jamar Adams and freshman Brandon Harrison, stepped into the breach when the two starters went down. And big Gabe Watson, all 300-some pounds of him, finally seemed motivated in the middle.

The analysts mention all these things. But is it possible that Herrmann also may be a much smarter and more adaptable defensive coordinator than he's been given credit for?

Herrmann's main area of responsibility has always been linebackers, the position he played for three years under Schembechler. That position also happens to be the part of the defensive structure showing the greatest improvement this year.

Herrmann has been the target, the guy everybody wants out. Before this season, a major criticism of Carr was that he was too loyal to Herrmann. The debt from 1997 had been paid in full, some fans said, and it was time to broom this guy and bring in someone with fresh ideas.

You heard it from the corner bar to the dorm rooms to the Victors Club tailgates. Herrmann was the designated villain when the 2005 season began.

What is he now?

Bye Week, November 5

If this were 1964, the season would be over already.

There were no byes back in that Rose Bowl year. The opener came on the last Saturday in September in those days, and the games went on for nine straight weeks, right up to Ohio State.

The next year the schedule expanded to 10 games, and in 1971 to 11. In 2006 there will be 12.

Yet the coaches and college presidents insist that a 10-game schedule with a two-game playoff within the bowl system would be too much for their student-athletes to handle.

Bushwa.

If you want to go way back, until 1942 Michigan played only an eight-game season. The schedule then was expanded to allow the wartime military teams—Great Lakes, Iowa Pre-Flight, and the rest—to schedule some games against the Wolverines. It then stayed at nine after the war was over.

In some of those seasons Michigan played only twice on the road. Seven out of the nine were at The Big House—none of this alternating home game stuff. Visiting teams knew the crowds would be much bigger in Ann Arbor than anything they could draw at home. So they cheerfully consented to come in every year.

Even into the 1950s, Michigan State would come to The Big House four years in a row before getting a return engagement. With Indiana, it was six years in a row. Purdue was rarely on the schedule back then, and in one stretch Michigan went 14 years, from 1948 to 1962, between games in West Lafayette.

Anyone who decries the fact that college sports have become just another business should examine those schedules. This was the bottom line talking more than 50 years ago.

But the bye week didn't arrive until Penn State joined the conference in 1994. That made 11 teams, and somebody had to be the odd one out one week every season.

Coaches have a love-hate relationship with the bye. It gives the lame and the halt a bit of time to recover. But if the team is in the middle of a streak, it also can break the momentum.

The infamous loss to Colorado in 1994 came off a bye week. So did losses to Illinois in 1999 and the wild 54–51 shootout against Northwestern in 2000, both of them ultimately costing the team Rose Bowl berths.

On the other hand, in the 1997 championship year the bye was the first week of the season. Every other Big Ten team already had played before Michigan got into game action on September 13. The team then went 11 straight weeks without breaking stride. The early bye didn't seem to hurt.

This team seems to have found its identity in the last three weeks of October. But the bye gives Hart and LaMarr Woodley—the best players on the roster on either side of the ball—a chance to recover. The starting safeties will also return, and maybe something will have clicked for Henne in the respite from weekly preparations.

Michigan is more than a three-touchdown favorite over Indiana next week, even though this seems to be a better Hoosiers team than most.

There is another odd quirk in the schedule this season. The last time Michigan finished the year with two straight home games was 1963. And the following season, the Rose Bowl year, they finished with two road games, including the conference-title clincher at Ohio State. Go figure.

The team's longtime equipment manager, Jon Falk, is still recovering from a broken leg. This was his 32nd season on the sideline, and he has become one of those institutions that Michigan finds so endearing.

He was in his accustomed place during the Iowa game when he was bowled over by a play that went out of bounds. Falk had to be carted off on a gurney and flown back to University Hospital in Ann Arbor.

A steady stream of former players paid him visits while he was laid up, even those who had long since graduated when he arrived on the scene.

One of these was Ron Kramer, the All-American end from the mid-1950s.

During Kramer's days in Ann Arbor, an elderly man would appear after every Thursday practice with a big basket of apples for the players. He became known as Mr. Apple, and the players of that era still talk about him.

So when Kramer paid his visit to Falk in the hospital, he brought along a basket of apples.

Falk knew of the tradition and appreciated the gesture. When Kramer left, though, one of the present-day Wolverines asked Falk who "the old guy with the apples" was.

"Son," Falk said, "if you're ever half the player that man was, you'll have accomplished something."

Michigan fans are more familiar with another long-standing tradition at The Big House. Whenever the opposing team gets into a fourth-down situation, the Michigan marching band starts to play "Temptation." The song even got a featured spot on the band's CD.

In all probability, no one in the stands much under the age of 60 has ever heard the song played in any other context. A good many of them may not even know its name. It's just another way to heckle the opposition.

Actually, "Temptation" has an interesting past. It was written in 1933 for one of Bing Crosby's first movies, *Going Hollywood*. Composed by Arthur Freed and Nacio Herb Brown, it was given a rather overwrought rendition, with Bing playing the role of a rejected lover staring disconsolately into his glass in a Mexican cantina and crooning this song with its insistent bolero beat. The song was a huge hit.

A cover of the song was recorded by George Olsen. His name is largely forgotten now, but during the late 1920s and early 1930s he led one of the most popular dance bands in America. He was also the first bandleader on the Jack Benny radio program.

But here's the twist. Olsen was also the first drum major in the history of the Michigan marching band. He was named to the position in 1914 and initiated the practice of flipping the baton over the goal post's crossbar and catching it on the far side.

Including the song in the Michigan band's repertoire is probably coincidental. Although maybe not. Michigan memories are long. Still, it wasn't introduced as a regular feature until the early 1950s, when arranger Jerry Bilik devised the band's rendition of the number, along with the other old warhorse, "The Hawaiian War Chant."

That was the era when the marching band really became the organization it is today. In many minds, the band is as much a part of a Saturday at The Big House as the game itself. When it comes stepping out of the Revelli Building—named for its director of 36 years, William B. Revelli—forms in the middle of Hoover Street, and goes into "The Victors," the day has truly begun.

It turns the corner onto Greene Street, a mass of bobbing shakos filling the entire width of the street, and then heads into the Victors' parking lot. At the base of the stairs to the stadium, it pauses to serenade the tailgaters with the fight song and then heads into the tunnel for its first appearance on the field.

In the unvarying pregame routine, it is when the band comes roaring out of the north end zone in the block M, blasting "The Victors" at full volume, with everyone in the stands joining in, that emotions reach their first peak of the day.

The years are peeled away and everyone is 20 again, getting ready to go out and face the world as conquering heroes. Those who have been away from The Big House for a while find their eyes filling with tears when they see it.

The band first began using the intricate formations for which it became famous in the 1920s. It wasn't called a marching band until 1936, and women were not permitted to join for another 36 years after that.

According to the official history of the band, in fact, it even formed a script Ohio on the field in 1932, before the first tuba player ever dotted the *I* in that formation for the Ohio State band.

It was in the late 1940s, however, that the band took its present form. Many of its arrangements were updated, and high-stepping marching techniques were brought in, including the 200-steps-a-minute entrance from the tunnel.

The emphasis may have shifted from a straightforward military style to a more rhythmic sort of presentation, but the sound and the appearance…they remain timeless.

Saturday Morning, November 12

"Illinois fans are the worst," says Bert Sampson. "Did you ever hear the outhouse story?"

Everyone else at the parking lot on the U-M Golf Course groans.

"Bert, at least wait until after we eat," says Jim Henry from the space two cars down. But Sampson will have none of that. He is into it.

"It was in the early 1980s against one of those Mike White teams," he says. "The feelings were bad between the schools back then because Bo thought Illinois gave Gary Moeller a raw deal. He felt White was taking advantage of the recruits that Moeller had brought in when he was head coach, and Mo never got any of the credit. He was also using a lot of junior-college transfers, and Bo didn't think too much of that, either.

"Well, we were up by six points late in the game at Champaign, and Illinois started driving the length of the field. They got a first down on our 4-yard line, and the crowd is going nuts. And we stop 'em on four straight plays. Michigan wins, 16–10.

"I get a little boisterous when that happens, and I'm all decked out in my maize-and-blue regalia. When I'm leaving the stadium, I got to pee real bad. So I go into one of the outhouses."

The others at the golf course tailgate are laughing already. The outhouse story is one of their favorites, and Sampson, who drives 150 miles each way to The Big House from Mecosta County, north of Grand Rapids, tells it well.

"I'm no sooner in there than the damn thing starts to rock. Some Illinois students had decided they were going to have some fun and tip it over with a Michigan fan inside. I try to get out, but they've bolted the door shut.

"It's rocking worse and worse, and the garbage from the hole starts sloshing around the floor. It's on my shoes and my socks and the bottom of my pants. And I've got this vision of the whole thing going over sideways and me drowning in a pool of shit."

By now, tailgaters from all down the row have walked over to hear Sampson tell the story one more time.

"Finally, my brother-in-law and some other guys come to my rescue. But I stink so bad they make me take off all the clothes on the lower part of my body before they let me in the car. And then, to cap it off, while we're stuck in traffic trying to get out of the parking lot, the sons of bitches stick an apple in the exhaust pipe and we stall out.

"Those Illinois fans. They're even worse than Ohio State."

All the tailgating SUVs are backed up to the edge of the grass. A few dozen feet away, tents have been set up to feed and entertain influential alumni and visiting groups of fans.

141

Like the Victors Club tailgaters in the lot across Stadium Drive, the golf course group fears the university is gradually encroaching on its space. At the Penn State game, there were so many tents set up, they came right down to the edge of the lot. The regulars were forced to find a parking space on the far side and hold their tailgates on concrete.

Calls were made, and they were assured that this would not happen again. But Ohio State is coming up in another week, and that always brings out the big shooters. If the university decides more and bigger tents are needed, where will that leave this bunch?

"We get here at 7:00 AM at the latest to stake out the spaces for the regulars," says Henry, who drives the 75 miles down from Metamora, in Lapeer County, with his buddy Eric Bechill. "No matter what the time of the game is…noon, 3:30 PM—we're here at 7:00 AM. My dog knows that Eric's car will be coming into our driveway at 5:40 AM.

"When we're a few minutes late, the guard here gets on our case. She knows her day begins when we show up."

Sampson has been parking here for 34 years, most of the others for around 20. Some are refugees from a lot near Schembechler Hall that was taken over by the university for a women's soccer field.

"We walked back to the car after the Ohio State game one year, and there was a little note stuck in the windshield telling us that we'd have to find somewhere else to park," says Tom Ryan, a longtime radio personality in Detroit. "That was warm [and heartfelt]. But we managed to get in here, and it's not a bad arrangement.

"The golf course attracts some interesting animals—and I'm not referring to us. One year we had a falcon perch in the tree right beside our tailgate table, and he dropped something right next to us. Turned out it was the carcass of the mouse he was eating. I guess he thought of it as his contribution to the tailgate."

Ryan drives to the game with his friend, Tom DeLisle, a Detroit-area journalist and television producer. DeLisle had radiation treatment for throat cancer during the summer, a procedure that damaged his salivary glands and sense of taste. He still can't take any solid nourishment, and his strength ebbs and flows. Aside from the opener, though, he has made every home game, hooking up an IV to the rear license plate of Ryan's SUV for his postgame meal.

"You go through something like this and you need encouragement from somewhere," he says. "Michigan football has been the one thing you could count on every year. They win, and you feel good.

"The start of this season wasn't real great therapy, though. And when you could see everything starting to crumble at the Penn State game—not just this season, but the whole edifice of Michigan football—it was almost unbearable. And when they pulled it out...look, I know how stupid this sounds, but I had tears in my eyes. It had become that personal, so connected to what I was going through myself.

"One thing I have learned [through] this experience, though. When you lose 50 pounds and let your hair grow long, you start to look like your mother."

It's a rather sparse tailgate this week for the Henry-Bechill group. They have been known to bring a satellite dish so they can pick up the pregame show on ESPN. They have also set up a portable generator so they can operate a pinball machine. After the game, other tailgaters usually gather around their SUV to check on the progress of other contests on their 20-inch TV screen.

But none of that stuff made the trip today. They're saving their big effort for next week and Ohio State.

"We like to try out new innovations every year," says Bechill. "We even got Bo one year. He was visiting one of the tents and came walking by and we asked him to pose with us by the TV set.

"He looked around and saw that we were getting cable and asked us how we were doing that. We pointed to the dish, and he just shook his head and said, 'I'll be a son of a bitch—now I've seen everything.'"

"My only complaint is that they televise every damn game now," says Bechill. (Actually, at the end of the 2005 season it will be 130 consecutive Michigan games on TV, which translates to 10 years straight on the tube.)

"It used to be you'd walk in that stadium and you felt like you were one of the privileged few. Maybe not so few with 100,000 people in there. But you know what I mean. Now everyone gets to see it in their own homes. I don't know. I think it detracts somehow."

"Hey, Bert," says DeLisle. "Tell us the Ohio State story."

"Oh, that's a good one," says Sampson. "A friend and I drive out to the Novi Hilton where Ohio State stays when they play here. We were in the maize and blue, and all the Buckeyes were razzing us.

"Finally, the team bus shows up late. Earle Bruce was the coach back then. He walks right past me and I say, 'Go Blue.' He turns his head, shoots me a glare, and just keeps walking, without a word.

"Well, I start thinking about this for a while. So I call the hotel operator and ask her to give me Bruce's room. She says she can't do that, and I say, 'Well, this is Earle Bruce Jr., and when my dad finds out that I'm stranded at the airport with no money and you wouldn't put me through to him, he's going to be pretty ticked off.'

"By then it's about midnight, and Bruce comes on the phone, kind of thick-voiced, and says 'Hello.' And I say, 'Go Blue, you son of a bitch,' hang up the phone, and run like hell."

"It's the running out of the hotel that gets me," says DeLisle. "Like he actually thought Bruce was going to come downstairs in his underwear and start chasing him."

It's an incredible morning for mid-November, part of this run of warm autumn weather.

"How do you beat this?" says Henry. "You know, people make a big deal about having seats on the 50-yard line. Our seats are in the end zone. But where do you see the greatest plays, the ones you talk about for years? The end zone! Those guys on the 50 are craning their necks to see what's going on, and it's happening right below our seats."

But what if it's happening at the other end zone?

"Hey, it's a 50-50 shot," says Henry. "But nothing historic ever happened at the 50-yard line."

You can't fight the logic.

10

November 12:
Michigan 41, Indiana 14

For once this season, it all goes right.

Michigan was a four-touchdown favorite at kickoff, and four it was at the close. Actually, it had 41 points by halftime and almost all the regulars took the last two quarters off. Even the walk-ons got into the action.

Hart did not play a single down, and Woodley was in for just a few. Carr said they could have played. But this was Indiana, and next week is...well, if you don't know what next week is, you're probably majoring in nerd.

It's funny how some universities play commendable basketball and hardly ever put together much of a football team.

Duke. Wake Forest. Kansas. Arizona. Kentucky.

If one were cruel, one might also add Michigan State to the list. Since MSU last went to the Rose Bowl, after the 1987 season, every other team in the Big Ten, except two, has won the conference title and gone to a BCS bowl.

The exceptions are Minnesota, which today became the latest team to plaster MSU, and Indiana. The Hoosiers, in fact, have been to a grand total of one major bowl in their entire history. It was the 1968 Rose, which they lost to O. J. Simpson and Southern California.

But their five NCAA basketball titles are far and away the best mark in the Big Ten. MSU is the only other conference team to win more than one. So maybe there's more truth than poetry in the basketball-school label.

The hot rumor of the day, incidentally, is that Smith will be out at MSU and replaced by Steve Mariucci, who will move to East Lansing from the Lions and rejoin his old Upper Peninsula high school buddy, Tom Izzo. Great rumor.

The game itself was a good deal less compelling. Indiana hasn't beaten Michigan since 1987, a result that turned several Hoosiers fans into dancing fools. The last time it won at Michigan was 1967—that damn year again. After winning three in a row at the start of the season, Indiana has dropped five of its last six. That made them a perfect warm-up act for the Buckeyes.

Still, when they took the opening kickoff and drove 77 yards on seven plays, there was some uneasy stirring. But that, as it turned out, was its offensive statement for the day.

On its first eight possessions, Michigan scored six touchdowns, missed a field goal, and was stopped on downs at the Indiana 8. Henne looked like his 2004 self again, picking out receivers all over the field and hitting them in stride instead of in their behinds.

But it was Grady and Breaston who were the revelations.

Grady, the much-advertised freshman tailback, finally looked comfortable. In previous games he seemed perplexed when the primary hole was closed. He had just run straight ahead instead of cutting back to find alternate running lanes.

This time, however, he was a force, bouncing to the outside decisively, wriggling free on a 32-yard touchdown run, and booming in on three straight inside carries from the 11.

Breaston, however, took over the game. By the end of the half, his all-purpose yardage was greater than that of Indiana's entire team. When the Hoosiers kicked off out of bounds— pretty good field position for Michigan at its own 35—Carr had them kick over. This time Breaston carried it to the Indiana 34—a net gain of 31 yards. That seemed to set the tone. Every time Indiana punted, Breaston eluded containment and reeled off returns that set up the Michigan offense in Hoosiers territory.

Once they even knocked him down before he could catch the ball. So after the 15-yard penalty, Henne threw to him for a 22-yard gain. Another time, they ran him on an end-around for 30 yards.

He was, once again, the game breaker he is supposed to be.

Carr also had a chance to reach deep into the bag and throw all sorts of tricks at the baffled Hoosiers. It's unlikely that any of these plays will be used against Ohio State. He just wanted to give Jim Tressel a little more to think about, maybe have him waste a little time in practice trying to defend against them.

The student section was in rollicking form, too—experimenting with different versions of the wave, hoisting fellow scholars to match the team's point total, and leaving en masse by the start of the fourth quarter. Too nice a day to sit still for a game that ended long ago.

There were scouts from the Alamo Bowl at the game. That is where the fourth-best team from the Big Ten goes. A few weeks ago, that would have seemed to be a worthy goal. Now Michigan has bigger things in mind. It would just as soon forget the Alamo.

"Penn State fans were the worst," says Sampson, back at the tailgate.

"I thought you said it was Illinois fans," says Ryan.

"Naw, it was those Penn State kids this year. They were yelling obscenities, giving us the finger all through that game. Throwin' stuff at the cheerleaders."

"The Michigan kids were throwing stuff during the Notre Dame game," says Henry.

"Yeah, but not at the cheerleaders," said Sampson. "And then Michigan scored that touchdown and that shut 'em up good. Damn Penn State fans."

"I think I counted 15 Indiana fans in the stands today," says DeLisle.

He may have underestimated, but only by a little. Even Northern Illinois seemed to bring in a larger contingent to The Big House. There was no solid block of red anywhere. You must get beaten down if you follow Indiana football consistently.

"Michigan wants everyone to wear blue next week," says Henry.

"That's the fad this season. Ever since Penn State beat Ohio State with everyone wearing white at the night game, that's the big thing. You got to show the colors."

"White isn't a color," says Bechill.

"Whatever," says Henry.

Why not dress everyone in maize next week? Probably because more Michigan fans own solid-blue sweatshirts and jackets. Besides, can you imagine a yellow wall, 100,000 bodies deep? It would not be a pretty sight.

So blue it is. And the final countdown is on.

Monday, November 14

"Did Michigan recruit me? Well, they told me I could come to a game."

Roger Zatkoff puts his head back and laughs. It's a big laugh, the kind you feel compelled to join. We are sitting in the kitchen of his suburban Detroit home over coffee and muffins and talking about what it means to play football for Michigan.

"I came out of Hamtramck High in 1949," he says, "and got a phone call. Illinois was interested, too. I had an uncle who played down there, and he intercepted a pass against Michigan that knocked them right out of the Rose Bowl in 1946. So they gave me a call out of the family connection.

"But I wanted to go to Michigan. So I thumbed it to Ann Arbor and stood at the entrance to the stadium tunnel like I was told. About 10 minutes before kickoff someone finally came out to get me. He led me onto the field, pointed into the stands, and said, 'Just sit wherever you want.' That was my big recruiting pitch. It was good enough for me."

Zatkoff played his final game for Michigan 53 years ago. But he has remained a constant presence in the alumni football association.

"Roger has done as much for this program as any former player," says association past-president Dave Rentschler. "Maybe not in terms of money. There are others who may have contributed more of that. But by his ability to impart the sense of what Michigan football means."

Compelling fact: Zatkoff is the only man to play for both a Michigan Rose Bowl team and a Detroit Lions championship team. He was a starter at linebacker in the 1951 bowl game at Pasadena and for the 1957 Lions.

But this week his thoughts are all with the Wolverines as they renew the ancient grudge against the Buckeyes. Along with the other Michigan stars from the past, he will be standing on the field he first entered long ago, right where the tunnel empties onto the turf, to form two parallel lines between which the 2005 Michigan team will run.

It's actually an idea that Michigan borrowed from OSU. But it is a wonderful sight, the symbolic passing of the torch from the old guard to the new.

"What did playing at Michigan mean to me?" he asks. "A part of your life that's always there. A symbol. Something that just keeps going on. We get together, regardless of the era, and we all connect. Instant friends. That ring on our fingers. God, I remember that last game I played for Michigan like it was yesterday. I never wanted it to end.

"You know, maybe the Ohio State game is a bigger deal now than it was back then," he says. "Of course, television and the rest of the media make everything seem bigger. The pitch is higher.

"But when I started at Michigan, we were at the top of the world. The last two teams had gone undefeated, national champions in 1948. We were the target for everyone. Ohio State was just the last game on our schedule. A big game, always. But for us it was just like playing Michigan State or Minnesota or Illinois. It meant everything to Ohio State, though. The only game that mattered."

Zatkoff is 74 now and is still vigorous even though the knee he tore up as a sophomore linebacker in 1950 still bothers him. It kept him out of his first Ohio State game, the infamous Snow Bowl. It also cut short his professional career at the age of 27. The house we are sitting in was built, for the most part, from money he earned as a pro. Zatkoff said the grand total for six years was $58,000.

"Now they have surgery that could have let me play more," he says. "Not back then. That's the only thing I regret."

The game he attended on his recruiting visit was not his first trip to The Big House.

"Back then the fence around the stadium was much lower than it is now," he says. "So my uncle would get a ticket and walk inside and my dad would stand outside and throw me over the fence. Then the three of us would sit down for the price of two.

"It was an interesting bunch of people on that first team. I was the baby of the group. We had guys who'd been in World War II. We have reunions of that Rose Bowl team from 1950 every five years, and I'm probably in the best shape of any of 'em.

"But it wasn't easy back then. I got married when I was still in school, and we had our first child in my senior year. I got paid $25 a month and free rent to manage this seven-unit apartment building in Ann Arbor. But that was a seven-day-a-week job, even on game days.

"Bennie [Oosterbaan] wanted us to all stay together at the university golf course the night before a game. So I'd have to get taped Saturday morning, run back to the apartment to stoke the furnace, and then run back in time for the game.

"The week before Ohio State in 1950 I banged up the knee in the Northwestern game. We got off to a bad start that year, lost to Michigan State and Army. But that was before MSU was in the conference, so it didn't hurt us too badly. We went into Ohio State with a loss and a tie in the Big Ten. We had to win and hope that Northwestern beat Illinois to get to the Rose Bowl.

"We spent the night before the game in a hotel in Toledo. Bennie didn't want us going into Columbus to stay. They'd do things like shut off the water at the hotel or stand outside yelling their heads off all night. Still do, I hear.

"By the time our train left the next morning, it was already snowing pretty heavy. The wind was howling, and even inside the train it was freezing. A patch of ice formed on the floor of the car, and we all just sat there and watched people slip as they came through, laughing our asses off. Bennie finally had to come back and tell us to cut it out.

"The train pulled in right next to the stadium in Ohio. I never thought they were going to play. They couldn't even get the tarp off the field at first. But they'd sold out the game, and I guess they didn't see any alternative. I was dressed, but I couldn't play because of the bad knee. My job was to pass out the hand warmers on the bench.

"It was so bad at times you couldn't see to the other side of the field. They called it the strangest game ever played. We won 9–3 on two blocked kicks, a touchdown, and a safety.

"I was able to get back in for the first half of the Rose Bowl. But I just didn't have the agility. I knew I couldn't play to my full capability, and at halftime I told the coaches to put in Ted Topor. We had to win this game. The Big Ten had never lost out there, and we weren't going to be the first to break the streak. I wasn't going to let ego get in the way.

"You always hear the Michigan coaches today stressing 'Team. Team.' But that's nothing new. It's always the way it's been there.

"My last game at Ann Arbor was against Purdue in 1952. We'd only lost one conference game and had to have this one. Someone on the staff came up to me in the locker room and said, 'Are you finally going to play a game for Michigan?' I ran after him and said, 'What are you talking about?' But he just walked away and wouldn't answer.

"I came out of that tunnel like a madman. I just beat the crap out of that poor kid from Purdue that day. One of the officials finally told me to loosen up. I asked him if I was doing anything illegal, and he said no. So I said to leave me alone, and I went right back at him. That poor kid never knew what hit him that day."

Another laugh. Another bite of muffin.

"Team was the motivator. But when you talk about motivation, the best was Bobby Layne. I only got in one season in Detroit with Bobby, but if he needed an extra effort from you on Sunday, he'd start in during practice and never let up.

"I'd come over during the off-season from Green Bay, where I played four years. I never moved my family up there for the season. Do you know what it was like to spend the entire season by yourself in Green Bay in the '50s? Not good. I saw marriages break up over that, and I wasn't going to let that happen to me.

"So I demanded a trade. I knew the Lions wanted a linebacker and hoped it would be there, my hometown. Instead, they sent me to Cleveland. I don't know why. They had some good, young linebackers on that team. But Paul Brown gave me a fair contract, and I spent the preseason there. I figured Cleveland was close enough to home.

"Then right at the end they traded me to the Los Angeles Rams. That did it. I told the commissioner's office I'd retire before I played out there. So the deal was voided and they set up a trade, instead, with the Lions—me for Lew Carpenter, the running back. And that's how I stumbled into the NFL championship.

"My favorite Bobby Layne story? I heard this second-hand from Frank Gatski, the center, who also had just come over from the Browns. Bobby got in the huddle and said, 'Gunner, when you and Harley [Sewell] get your blocks figured out on this play, I want the one who's free to help the tackle on your side. He needs some help.'

"Well, that tackle was Lou Creekmur, who is only in the Pro Football Hall of Fame. He started yelling at Layne, but Bobby glared at him and said, 'I'm not talking to you. Gunner, just do what I say.'

"Needless to say, nobody got past Creekmur the rest of that game. But that was Bobby. He knew exactly when to jab in the needle.

"Of course, you heard the story about halftime in our playoff game with San Francisco. They had us 24–3, and the walls between the locker rooms at Kezar Stadium were paper thin. [Editor's note: The halftime score was actually 24–7.] We could hear them yelling and saying how they were going to spend their checks for the championship game. No one on our side had to say a word. We went out and took it to 'em, 31–27. Then we just destroyed Cleveland, 59–14. The guys on defense all said we didn't earn our paychecks that day because our offense was unstoppable."

He sips the coffee, and another memory returns.

"One more thing. When Ron Kramer was playing for Green Bay. We never were together at Michigan or the Packers, and he ended up with the Lions, too. But one game he was playing tight end up there and I was at linebacker, and we just whaled the daylights out of each other. My God, that was fun. Just beat the snot out of each other, two old Michigan guys going at it.

"Today's athletes are far superior to what we were. It's all just evolved in terms of conditioning. But the emotional component...that doesn't change. When you play at Michigan, you're always the target. The biggest game on everyone else's schedule. They all want to get you. You have to learn how to expect that and prepare yourself.

"Everybody has different ways of focusing themselves on the game. But when you come down that tunnel at Michigan Stadium and you hear the roar start to build...maybe it's something you have to experience yourself. You can't really describe that emotion.

"You know, football is a game of physical force. But you've also got to think. What's the pressure of the block this guy is giving me? Is he setting up a screen, a draw, a sweep? Every play you've got to process that information instantly and then react.

"It's such a wonderful game. I only wish I could have played forever."

Wednesday, November 16

If you don't have a reservation yet, forget about it.

No, not to The Big House. You can always speak purposefully to a scalper on State Street for that kind of ticket. But all across this great land, wherever Michigan alumni reach critical mass, they will be gathering Saturday to watch it together. The Ohio State game is just too gut-churning to go through alone. It must be a communal experience.

So by midweek, sports bars from Boston to Hawaii have sold out their reservations for the game.

It's not enough merely to have a reservation. If you want a good table, you'll have to show up hours before kickoff. Before the tailgaters in Ann Arbor even unpack their gear and fire up the barbecue, the far-flung contingent will be waiting in line.

"I know from experience that for a noon kickoff Chicago time, we'd better be in line at Duffy's by 8:00 AM," says Tina Smith, a 1999 graduate of Michigan. "The doors don't open until 10:00. But I've got a group of 15 going, and if we want to stay together, that's the drill."

It's become customary in recent years to refer to fans of a certain team who are now scattered across the land as a "Nation." Devotees of the Boston Red Sox may have been the first to describe themselves in this fashion, but it's caught on in many places.

The term addresses a certain reality in American life. People don't stay in one place anymore.

They grow up here, go to college there, and work somewhere else. But there are certain loyalties, usually fashioned in youth, that aren't as easily changed as an address.

A kid from Connecticut who grew up with a passion for the Red Sox is not likely to turn into a Mariners fan just because his job takes him to the Pacific Northwest. Likewise the young woman from Pittsburgh who went to Steelers games and waved a towel with her dad probably will not be a big Dolphins fan just because she now lives in Fort Lauderdale. Usually, but not always, these Nations consist of transplants from older cities who have found a more comfortable sort of life in the Sun Belt.

Michigan football, however, may be a special case.

Among the public institutions in America, only the University of Vermont has a higher percentage of out-of-state students. Fully one-third of the entering class at Ann Arbor in any given year is from somewhere other than Michigan.

A large number come from the Chicago and New York areas. While these people grew up there and retain fierce loyalties to da Bears or the Yankees, their hearts glow maize and blue. Many of them, especially males from the East Coast, may choose Michigan deliberately because of its big-time sports programs.

They crave The Big House experience. Any comparable program in the East is pretty much limited to Penn State. So for the combination of academics and athletics, they head to Ann Arbor.

On this Saturday, the New York contingent will gather at the Park Avenue Country Club, between Murray Hill and

Union Square, where so many of Manhattan's bright young things reside.

In Boston they'll assemble at The Place, right off Government Center. In San Francisco it'll be at the Bayside, on Union Street. In the Los Angeles area, at Gotham Hall, on Santa Monica's Third Street. The game will not be shown on network TV in California and can be picked up only with a satellite dish, so these gatherings are not to be regarded as frills. Even in Honolulu, where kickoff will be at 8:00 AM local time, they will wipe the sleep from their eyes and assemble at the Eastside Grill.

There will even be some brave souls who will meet in the belly of the beast to cheer on the Wolverines. The Michigan Club of Greater Cincinnati will gather for the game at Willie's Bar and Grill, in the suburb of Kenwood.

"We'll have about 200 people in here for that one," says manager Mike La Liberte. "We've even got some people who'll come in here to watch the Lehigh-Lafayette game on satellite.

"And in another part of the room, we'll have the Ohio State fans."

How's that again? Putting such people in the same room? Wouldn't that, perhaps, be considered foolhardy, if not making one an accessory to manslaughter?

"Oh, we don't anticipate problems," says La Liberte. "You'll notice that we're a grill as well as a bar. We serve lots of food, and that seems to calm things down."

In Chicago, though, the Michigan troops, about 400 strong, will have the place all to themselves, without any competition from Buckeyes or those crazy fools from Lafayette.

Duffy's, on Diversey Parkway, was established in 2000 by an entrepreneur with strong University of Michigan ties. He sold out four years later, but it has remained the gathering place for Wolverines, many of them transplanted from the Detroit area. Like accountant Tina Smith.

"It'll be crazy in there," she says. "They'll be playing 'The Victors,' and everyone will be wearing Michigan shirts. You'll see people you haven't seen since the last Ohio State game.

"The first few years I lived here, everyone my age showed up for every game. Now it's a younger crowd. I guess that's the natural progression. But Ohio State is different. It's a reunion as much as a football party."

The same will be true at Tavern on the Tracks, in Charlotte. And at The Pour House, just down from the Capitol in D.C. And at The Line, in Atlanta.

Wherever the Nation has settled in, this is the week it gathers.

Friday, November 18

Every season begins in bright promise. And each one leads here, to this game, traditionally played beneath a glowering November sky.

This is not a game that lends itself to sunshine. Leave that for Alabama-Auburn or Southern Cal–UCLA. This is a game rooted in late midwestern autumns, long after Indian summer has gone and the bleak business of winter is at hand. Even when the sun does come out, it is a cold shining.

Both teams recruit across the country. Their rosters contain plenty of kids from Florida and California. But in this game, the shadow of the steel mills and the auto plants, the historic soul of Ohio and Michigan, falls across the field. Football is again reduced to its elemental core.

There were traces of snow on the ground this week after a violent wind and rain storm brought in the first Canadian front of the season. It may have been shirtsleeves for Indiana, but the forecast says parkas for OSU. Who would want it any other way? This is how it's supposed to be.

An ESPN poll named Michigan–Ohio State as the greatest sports rivalry in existence. There are those who would claim that title for Yankees–Red Sox baseball or even Duke–North Carolina basketball. With all due respect, they are out of their minds, or at the very least guilty of rank provincialism.

The Red Sox and the Yankees will play each other well over a dozen times over the course of a single season. The Tar Heels and Blue Devils will meet two or three times. But for Michigan and Ohio State, all that has gone before in their seasons is prologue. This one game is everything. Sixty minutes of turmoil.

Entire books have been written about the history of this game. It is always at the end of the season and, in many instances, the end of a career.

Coaches who can't beat Michigan—Wes Fesler, John Cooper—generally have a short shelf life in Columbus. Their job becomes a misery. The mailman delivers diatribes. Night visitors place "For Sale" signs on their front lawns.

Michigan generally has a higher tolerance for such failure. But when Bump Elliott ended the 1968 season with a 50–14 evisceration at OSU's Horseshoe, he was toast. And that came in an 8–2 season, too. But it was the second time Hayes had run up 50 on Elliott, and it was too much to bear.

The classic example of how fortune can turn was Francis A. Schmidt. He arrived in Columbus in 1934 and endeared himself to the Buckeyes by originating one of the great sports clichés—the one about Michigan being just like everyone else and putting on their pants "one leg at a time." When he followed that up by shutting them out, OSU instituted the tradition of handing out tiny gold pants to the players on teams that won this game.

Schmidt followed his debut with three more shutouts, the longest and most complete stretch of OSU dominance in the history of the series. But in 1938 Michigan brought in Fritz Crisler as head coach, and things were reversed immediately. Crisler won three straight times, the last one a 40–0 walloping in Columbus. Schmidt was told to take his pants and scram.

The start of the current era of Michigan football is always dated from the 1969 upset of OSU, the first time Bo Schembechler took on Woody Hayes. Michigan had gone 5–12 against the Buckeyes under Hayes. He said afterward that this was his best team ever in Columbus, the defending national champions, unbeatable on both sides of the ball.

It was the start of a reinvigorated Michigan program. Over the next six years, its overall record was 58–6–3. But four of those losses and one of the ties came at the hands of Hayes, and each one was more maddening than the last. Four straight times, Michigan took a perfect record into the game only to be thwarted.

The 10–10 tie in the 1973 game, when OSU was ranked number one, was especially galling. The Big Ten athletics directors voted to reverse their own tradition and send the Buckeyes to the Rose Bowl for the second straight year, even though the teams had tied for the championship. The injustice was so profound that it resulted in the end of the conference ban on playing in other bowls. And more than 30 years later, talking about the vote still enrages Schembechler.

Not until 1976 did Michigan become the truly dominant team in the series, going 9–5 for the rest of Schembechler's tenure.

Even in those rare instances when neither team is a factor in the conference race, this is still the game both sides must win. But the very rarest of treats is when one of them can spoil an entire season for the other. It is understood at OSU that if given the choice between a 10–1 season with the loss coming to Michigan and a 1–10 year with the reverse result, the second option would be preferred.

In 1995 and 1996 Michigan took on second-ranked Ohio State teams and beat them both times. The second instance probably cost Ohio the national championship.

Carr went 5–1 in his first six shots at OSU. But in 2002 OSU came into Ann Arbor and dislodged Michigan from a Rose Bowl bid. That was Tressel's first year at Columbus, and since his arrival it has been a 3–1 OSU advantage. His unranked team in 2004 shredded Michigan's national ranking and took much of the luster from its season with a 37–21 walloping, part of the team's late defensive collapse.

The final decision this year won't come until after the game is over. In East Lansing, Penn State takes on MSU as a seven-point favorite. Should the 5–5 Spartans inexplicably pull themselves together, it would then be the winner of this game that goes to the BCS bowl as Big Ten champions.

Even without the bowl possibilities, the scenario is rich.

Vengeance. Redemption. Pride. Passion.

The usual stuff.

The Fire Lloyd bloggers have fallen silent. Instead, Carr is being lauded for his refusal to panic in the face of three demoralizing losses. With the very real chance of a losing season only one second away, he kept the team in the Penn State game, and it all turned around. Now they are 7–3.

If he can somehow pull this off, it will be one of the greatest comebacks in school history.

At Michigan, it is simply accepted as fact that Ohio State fans are one step removed from the great apes. And not a very large step, at that.

Everyone has a story involving abuse and maltreatment in Columbus—from the fire engines parked in front of the team hotel employing their sirens at regular intervals through the night to the targeting of Michigan plates by the Ohio Highway Patrol on U.S. 23, the main route into Columbus from the north, to the contumely incurred by anyone who employs either blue or maize in their wardrobe while out for a stroll on High Street.

But in 2004 the Buckeyes outdid themselves.

As the Michigan players walked from the team bus to the stadium entrance, they were told by university security, accompanied by slobbering police dogs, to place their duffel bags on the ground so they could be inspected for weapons of mass destruction. Those who hesitated were yelled at.

Carr could barely control his anger over this breach of protocol. Could OSU security seriously believe that one of his players was part of a plot to blow up The Horseshoe? Or, more likely, was this simply part of a psychodrama intended to throw the favored team off its game?

If that was the case, it succeeded handily. Even a year later, Carr was clearly miffed. This abuse went beyond the acceptable.

Michigan fans, as everyone knows, are holy and pure and would never resort to such tactics. Except, perhaps, for Sampson yelling, "Go Blue, you son of a bitch," into Bruce's hotel telephone at midnight. And Grossman mocking George to some elderly OSU fans during the 1995 game. Maybe one or two other little incidents over the long sweep of time.

But all season-ticket holders were sent emails this week, reminding them to be courteous and play nice and to leave their police dogs at home.

OSU is a three-point favorite. Since its defeat at Penn State, it has utterly destroyed everything in its path.

Isn't this how it's supposed to be?

Saturday Morning, November 19

So much of the sweetness of the college football season lies in its brevity.

It began at The Big House only 12 weeks ago, and now the annual circle already is closing.

Pro football has another month and a half to run and then starts the playoffs. Hockey and basketball, both underway now, will go almost to the start of summer. There is still some college football to be played at other venues, and there will be a bowl game for Michigan somewhere warm. But in Ann Arbor, this is the last.

That is why the sense of high anticipation that runs through all the streets of the city today is tinged with a sense of regret.

It could well be the last party ever at the famous Jaffe-Lester tailgate before the university takes over their little hillock. This senior class will have moved on by the time they tee it up again next year. They will return to The Big House in May to get their diplomas and then leave for the real world. For others in the stands, only too aware of the years passing, this may be the last game they will attend.

This will definitely be the last for Howard King. The veteran public-address announcer, who had to miss the opener because of illness, said this week that he could not continue. The drive down from his new home in Traverse City seven weekends a year has become too difficult.

Sampson says this may be it for him, too, because of the long drive and the mounting expense of license fees and tickets. There are more good-byes among those who see each other only at these games, through adjacent tailgate spaces or seats. Strong friendships are struck up during the season and won't be picked up again for nine months. They wish each other a Merry Christmas and a Happy New Year. They might as well throw in Easter and the Fourth of July, too, because they won't meet again until September.

The great line from Rolf Humphries poem "Polo Grounds" applies at The Big House, too: "The man in the stands grows older every year. The players are forever young."

Forever young. Just kids, really. How foolish it is to stake one's sense of well-being on the arm of a 19-year-old or on the back of a kid who just became eligible to buy a beer. Part of you must remain forever young as well in order to suspend exterior reality and do that. That in itself is a comforting thought.

Down in Virginia, incidentally, Liberty University announced today that it is firing its football coach, who has a 1–9 record. This is the same institution attended by blogger DeSantis, who was so fired up to fire Carr earlier this fall. It seems that he was just a little confused about the right target.

The day has come with a surprising turn in the weather. The skies decline to glower. There is sunshine and temperatures in the upper 40s, a good seven to 10 degrees warmer than predicted. No hint of the cold rain or snow that was also forecast.

Still, people are dressed in layers. Some are wearing boots, and the drink of choice is hot coffee.

The band approaches the stadium, salutes everyone with one more chorus of "The Victors," and moves into the tunnel. As if awaiting this cue, the tailgaters also begin heading toward the gates, bunching up once more to hand in their tickets and open their coats for inspection, and then doing it a second time at the entrance to their section. Today it feels good to be herded close, and not only to ward off the cold.

The stadium clocks tick down the seconds to kickoff. Mike Ben and Gene Rontal lean forward from their prime seats. The golf course tailgaters peer out from the end zone. Mark Snyder sorts through his game-day notes in the press box. At Moe's, the TV on the wall beams unwatched to an empty selling floor. At Duffy's and Willie's and Gotham Hall, the expatriates maneuver to get the best view of the TV from their tables. In homes all over the country, the same urgent sense of expectancy rises.

The ball is in the air. The game is on one more time.

November 19:
Ohio State 25,
Michigan 21

D octor, I keep having this dream. A nameless dread is approaching, drawing nearer and nearer. I know I should do something to stop it, but I can't. I'm paralyzed. My muscles won't react. It's terrifying. What should I do?"

"Maybe you should turn in your Michigan tickets."

"What! And give up all that fun?"

A waitress at Sunny's Café in West Bloomfield spots a man in an Ohio State baseball cap, the kind Woody Hayes used to wear, sitting by himself.

"He's lucky I don't spill coffee in his lap," she mutters. She is wearing a maize Michigan T-shirt.

In Como's Restaurant in Ferndale, Marc Dwoskin, DDS, spots a man in the full red regalia.

"Oh, Aitch," yells the doctor.

"Eye, Oh," answers the other diner, and they shake hands.

"I didn't go to OSU, but I grew up in Ohio," says Dwoskin. "I just like to make a living off my friends by betting against Michigan every year in this game. They're so damn arrogant."

Not every scenario has a happy ending, and not every landing is soft. What we have here is a season that went in a circle.

All the questions asked at its beginning remain unanswered at its end.

With seven minutes left in the game, OSU came from nine points down to score two easy touchdowns and beat Michigan for the fourth time in five years. And for the fourth time in Michigan's last five losses, going back to last season's Rose Bowl, it happened because the defense couldn't get off the field when it absolutely had to.

Texas, Wisconsin, Minnesota, Ohio State—all games lost in the last seconds, three of them with Michigan defending a lead. Even in two of this year's wins—Penn State and Iowa— the defensive unit gave up critical points at the end. Only a last-second touchdown pass and an overtime touchdown run averted those calamities.

In every instance, the defense played well until it had to make a stop, and then it couldn't.

The statistical improvement is impressive. Only Michigan State broke 30 on the Wolverines, and that was a defeat for them. But, as is often said, stats are for losers. The defense couldn't seal the deal in any close game.

So Michigan fans are learning to deal with an entirely alien brew—the battery acid cocktail of resignation.

"You couldn't even get angry," said Ben. "You could just see it coming. All we could do was look at each other and say, 'Let's hope there's enough time left on the clock for us to come back.' But there wasn't."

"This was a 7–4 team that played like a 7–4 team," said Bershad on the dark and somber drive home. "I hear people say that it could just as easily have been a 10–1 team, and they even had a chance to pull out the Notre Dame game. But as far as I'm concerned it could just as easily have been a 4–7 team, too. Honestly, they were lucky to finish with a winning season, and I can't remember the last time I said that about Michigan."

"We stared in numbness after the final drive and left the stadium as quickly as we could, which wasn't quick enough," said DeLisle. "What is the *point* of the 'Bend and Break' defense? God damn it, one blitz…just one sack…and they could have changed the rhythm of that final drive. But no, they stood around and watched them go without ever once getting in their way. A disgrace.

"To make it even better, one staggering drunk guy in a Buckeyes jersey vomited all over our section in the first quarter. It just seemed to punctuate the day. We'll get over the game, but never that fat idiot exploding in the aisle. Such a metaphor for the final outcome."

Michigan had one break after another fall into its lap today. A missed extra point, critical interference and holding penalties on OSU, a shanked punt deep in OSU territory, and a fumble by quarterback Troy Smith in the same part of the field. One of OSU's star linebackers, Bobby Carpenter, went down on the first play of the game.

But all the old Michigan injuries returned under the incessant pounding of this game. Mike Hart. Jake Long. Tim Massaquoi. LaMarr Woodley. All of them had to go out. At one point, the entire starting offensive line was gone. Leo Henige broke his leg, and center Adam Kraus spent the entire day on the sideline.

Injuries are also an excuse for losers.

The running game was nonexistent, and while Henne may have played his finest game of the year, he couldn't do it alone. OSU was too good to be beaten by such a one-dimensional offense. They were clearly the better team.

The Sunday *Detroit News*, with its gift for the felicitous headline, called the loss "Heartbreaking." It was hardly that. More like heartburn.

People were so dispirited there weren't even any new calls to fire Carr or Herrmann. That will surely come. Columnists who can't think of anything else to write can always fall back on demanding someone's job. Funny how they react when someone threatens theirs, though.

"They were 8–4 my last two years in college, and when I come back home, they're probably going [to be] 8–4 again," said Ben. "It's as if I never left home."

The circle had closed.

Sunday, November 20

When he got home Saturday night, Elliott Parr went through the usual ritual.

He took the scrapbook down from its place over the television set in his study. Then he carefully slid the Ohio State game ticket into its slot between the plastic covers.

Now the season was officially complete. Another one was preserved for posterity.

"I started saving these tickets in 1980," he says. "I'd been going to games long before that, and if you ask me why 1980, I can't explain it. Maybe I'd just reached a point in my life where it became important to keep things.

"So I take the stub of every Michigan game, regular season and bowls, that I went to and keep it in this book. I've been to a lot."

Parr doesn't consider himself a collector. He doesn't go after the more elaborate memorabilia, like the stuff you'll find in Jaffe's basement. Nor does he seek out the arcane. It's just ticket stubs and some player cards. Well, a lot of cards, actually. Michigan football players. Michigan football players in their pro uniforms. Michigan baseball players who turned pro. Michigan basketball players who did the same. Barry Larkin and Jim Abbott. Cazzie Russell and Glen Rice.

"Maybe it's that I can't bring myself to throw anything away that has the block M on it," he says. "And I didn't even go to Michigan. I graduated from Wayne State. But Michigan was my dad's team, and when you go to the games with your father, they become your team, too.

"I once was on a plane from Chicago and found myself sitting next to Lloyd Carr. I'm not the kind of guy who runs up to celebrities, and I knew he just wanted to sit there and be left alone to read his newspaper. But I had to call my dad and tell him who was sitting next to me.

"Then I asked Lloyd if he would mind saying hello to my dad. He took the phone without missing a beat and said, 'Mr. Parr, I've been sitting next to your son for 15 minutes and he's already trying to tell me who I should start at quarterback.' My dad told him not to pay any attention to me. He still gets to the games, and he's in his upper 80s."

The oldest ticket in Parr's book is the 1948 Rose Bowl. Michigan 49, Southern California 0. Cost: $5.50.

The most recent was the 2005 Rose Bowl. Texas 38, Michigan 37. Cost: $125.

One Rose Bowl ticket isn't kept in the book. Parr has the 1998 stub mounted in a glass frame along with the front page of the *Free Press* with the headline reading "Hail, Yes!!" Michigan 21, Washington State 16. The national title game. Cost: beyond rubies.

"I drove in from Palm Springs for that game first thing in the morning because I didn't want to miss a minute of the day," he says. "I've never been so nervous before a game. I had two tickets, and one of them was for seat number 18. Maybe I'm a little superstitious, but the 18th is my birth date. And the number 18 is the symbol of life for Jewish people. So I knew I had to use that one."

Here is the ticket to a tough loss to Notre Dame in 1989. It sits in the casing upside down.

"I put in all the losses upside down," says Parr. "It's like a signal of distress, and it helps me remember what the game was about, too.

"This one here was from a game in South Bend. Here's a couple from Northwestern, Illinois, a few from Michigan

State. This one is from a regular-season game in the Rose Bowl against UCLA. Beat 'em on a field goal with one second to play. That was beautiful."

Up until 1993 the tickets were much wider with lots of colorful action art on them. But then they narrowed down to the size of theater stubs. It must have saved a lot of trees, a popular move at a place like Michigan.

"There's still a theme for the tickets every year," says Parr. "One year it was great players, one year it was rivalries. This year it was all coaches—back to Fielding Yost. My dad's favorite was Harry Kipke from the 1930s."

Kipke is probably the least remembered of the national championship coaches, although the street that leads into the Victors' parking lot is named for him.

In 1993 tickets sold for $25 a game. By 1998 they were up to $32, and then $49. This season they came in at $59, along with the $500 license fee.

"I don't even think twice about renewing," he says. "I'd give up a lot of other things before that. I'll never not go.

"You know, my company buys season tickets to a lot of teams in the Detroit area. Most of them we give away for business reasons, to customers and suppliers. But not the Michigan tickets. That's always been our family time together.

"People call Michigan fans arrogant. I don't mind that. In fact, I'll agree with them. We've got a lot to be arrogant about. Look at the record. Besides, if you run a clean program and your team is in contention for the Big Ten title every year— and we were, right up to the last game this season—maybe it's not really arrogance. Maybe it's just reality.

"A bunch of us played golf this morning. I can never remember doing that the morning after an Ohio State game. It's just been an incredible autumn.

"We started talking about next year. The schedule doesn't look good. We get Notre Dame, Penn State, and Ohio State all on the road. So already some of the guys are getting down about 2006.

"But did you see how many starters will be coming back? Henne and Hart will be better. The redshirts are supposed to be incredible. Because of all the injuries on the offensive line a lot of the younger guys got in playing time, and we can't possibly have a run of injuries like that two years in a row.

"You know, Michigan teams seem to do better when less is expected of them. Look at '97. No one predicted a championship for that team. So maybe things won't be so bad after all in 2006.

"And maybe that's the key. Whatever else happens, with Michigan there's always something to look forward to."

There are plenty of open slots left in Parr's ticket book, too.

12

December 28: Alamo Bowl
Nebraska 32, Michigan 28

I t turned out those bowl scouts from San Antonio, the guys who were skulking around the Michigan press box during the Indiana game, were right on the money.

As unimpressive as their 7–4 record may have been, it should have earned the Wolverines a trip to Tampa to play Florida on New Year's Day in the Outback Bowl.

Instead, that bowl chose Iowa, a team that finished with the same conference record as Michigan and had lost to them.

The unstated reason was that Outback Bowl officials felt Iowa fans were more likely to travel there and buy tickets.

This was a staggering admission. One of the props of Michigan's reputation is that it has the largest and most mobile fan base in college football. Now even that was being dissed.

It all seemed to be part of the same malaise that overlaid this entire season, a slow and sickening plunge from the heights. Three home losses. WJR checks out on radio coverage. Now even a second-tier bowl doesn't want them. This can't be good.

Nevertheless, the Outback's reasoning was sound. After two straight trips to the Rose Bowl, it seemed unlikely that lots of Michigan fans would want to settle for a journey to Tampa. So the team fell to the next level, the Alamo Bowl. It was the first time in 10 years that Michigan would not play in January.

It turned out to be a self-fulfilling prophecy. If Michigan fans were reluctant to fly to Florida, they sure as hell weren't about to go to Texas.

There is a strong connection between Michigan and Florida, with thousands of alumni vacationing or owning a second home or retiring there. Texas, on the other hand, is Texas.

So only a handful of them made the trip to San Antonio, while fans from Nebraska packed the Alamodome. They turned entire sections of the stands into blocks of bright red, a reasonable facsimile of a Saturday afternoon in Lincoln. The Cornhuskers, a 10½-point underdog, also seemed to want it more. Their long string of winning seasons had ended in 2004, leaving Michigan as the owner of the longest such streak in college football. This was to be a redemptive trip for Nebraska. For Michigan it was a consolation prize, and a pretty sorry one at that.

The game also turned out to be a microcosm of the Michigan season. It could finish on neither side of the ball. Chances to take control of the game were squandered, including a close-in missed field goal, an interception in the Nebraska end zone, a fumble on the 17 that gave Nebraska its winning touchdown, and the inability to get it in from the 20 in the last two minutes. And once more the defense was able to stop the opposition on every possession, except the one when it had to.

After 12 games it was still a team that had no identity and did not know how to win.

The worst officiating crew in the history of college football did not help matters. Drawn from the Sun Belt Conference, the zebras seemed overwhelmed by the speed of the game. It sure wasn't like this at Middle Tennessee State. It all ended in a fiasco, with the Nebraska bench pouring onto the field to celebrate while the final play, a series of laterals to trailing backs, was still alive. No penalty was called. That was probably an act of mercy.

But winners take Gatorade showers, and losers complain about the officiating.

The entire mess took four hours to play. There were moments when it seemed that Michigan was trying to stretch it out long enough to play on New Year's Day, after all.

The papers called it another "heartbreaking loss." But they may have placed the break a little too high on the anatomy.

Afterword

February 12, 2006

The first to go was Terry Malone.

Rumors had been bubbling for the last six weeks on the blogs, among the blabbermouths on sports talk radio, even in permanent print. The long-awaited shakeup on the staff of assistant coaches was coming. From the day after the Alamo Bowl, it was topic A.

The question was, would it merely mark the official end to a truly calamitous season, or could this be the start of something big?

Because enough was already too much. After the worst season in 21 years, things had to change. You can't turn your head and pretend that 7–5 is an optical illusion.

When another of the elite programs, Miami, also finished its season at a lesser bowl, the Peach, and was absolutely pasted there, 40–3, Head Coach Larry Coker fired four assistants with a combined total of 59 years in the program. Even Assistant Head Coach Art Kehoe, who had been part of the staff for all five of the Hurricanes' national titles since 1983, was let go. Miami had won the title as recently as 2001 and lost it in overtime the following year. But the message was clear. This sort of result is unacceptable, and if this staff can't deliver, Coker will find one that can.

But the word throughout the college football world is that a job at Michigan is long on security and short on accountability.

But you can count up the injuries to the entire offensive line and to Hart and Woodley and half the defensive backfield…and it still didn't add up. This was not a 7–5 team. The strange thing is it could just as easily have gone 12–0 as 4–7.

There was an apparent touchdown against Notre Dame waved off when the officials refused to order up a replay. A momentum-changing late fumble at Wisconsin. Inexplicable defensive brainlock in the final minute against Minnesota. Two seconds returned to the clock to beat Penn State. Anal play selection by Iowa and Michigan State when both teams had the chance to win those games in regulation. Last possession breakdowns against Ohio State and Nebraska.

When outcomes are decided by such small margins, it's hard to make sense of them. But Malone was the first to go, after a decent interval had elapsed.

First things had to come first. January is recruiting time, leading up to Signing Day on February 1, when oral intentions are put on the dotted line.

The people who rank this sort of thing gave the Wolverines their typical high grades. Thirteenth nationally, top three in the Big Ten. One question: if these people have the ability to project with such assurance how high school kids are going to perform in actual college competition, why aren't they all living in the Caribbean and lighting cigars with $20 bills from their gains on Wall Street?

No one knows. Like all the football rankings, they're just numbers floating around in space.

Matt Gutierrez, who never lost a game as a high school quarterback, is gone. Named as the starter, he could never get the job back from Henne after going down with a shoulder injury just days before the 2004 season began. He is transferring to Idaho, in the WAC, a wide-open offensive conference, and will remain one of the great might-have-beens in Michigan history.

Max Martin has also departed. He inherited the tailback job when Hart went down but fumbled it away to freshman Grady. Carr called him one of the most impressive running backs ever to come to Michigan on his Signing Day. Now he's gone to impress the coaches at Alabama, his home state.

But the new arrivals were definitely the secondary story this year. The larger question was who would be there to coach them?

Malone would not. The week after Signing Day he turned in his resignation.

He was a local guy. Played at Catholic Central in Detroit before going on to star at Holy Cross as a tight end. Prior to being named coordinator in 2002, his specialty was turning out great offensive linemen. That was his job on the 1997 team, and three of his starters on the 2001 squad were drafted by the NFL midway through the second round.

Michigan traditionally builds from the offensive line. It is chapter one, verse one of the Book of Bo. But that always seems to lead to a conservative mind-set among coaches steeped in this doctrine. The fans want thunder and lightning. They thought they knew where to find it, too.

Loeffler was their man. He groomed the quarterbacks who had given wings to the Michigan attack. Although it remained a team that always ran first to set up the pass, it now turned to the pass more often than ever before. John Navarre set all kinds of records at Michigan simply because he was given the chance to put it in the air more frequently than any of his predecessors. The 31-year-old Loeffler was the young prodigy who made it all work.

But after Malone's departure to the New Orleans Saints was announced, Carr named DeBord to take over his old job as offensive coordinator.

The move had been telegraphed for months, ever since DeBord returned from Central Michigan before the 2004 season. He and Carr are tight. In the head coach's mind, much of the credit for spinning the modestly talented offense of 1997 into championship gold went to DeBord. It is also a matter of unspoken understanding that this is the man Carr will choose to replace him when he finally moves into an administrative position. That is, if he is given that choice.

But DeBord's background, like Malone's, comes off the offensive line. That's what he did in his first coaching job at Michigan when Moeller hired him in 1992, and it was where he had played for four years at little Manchester College in Indiana. To the commentators, it looks like just more of the same.

To add to the fun, Loeffler was seen having dinner with Tom Brady, one of his closest friends, during Super Bowl week in Detroit. Stories immediately circulated that Loeffler was going to interview with the Patriots for the same job he held at Michigan and be reunited with his old pal.

When the smoke settled, however, Loeffler denied that he was going anywhere. He would remain at Michigan as quarterbacks coach. While that was not the resolution his advocates had hoped for, it still was better than losing him altogether. It was regarded as an acceptable outcome.

No sooner had that been settled, though, when the defensive situation blew up. Two days after Malone's resignation, English announced he'd be moving on to coach the defensive backs at the Chicago Bears.

This could reasonably be described as a bombshell. To the growing anti-Herrmann brigades, it was more than that. It was a sign of the end of days.

The bright young mind was leaving, and all that was left was what they had already seen. This time the outcry even penetrated the thick walls of Schembechler Hall.

Carr realized that he could not bring back Herrmann as the defensive coordinator for another year—not after all those fourth-quarter collapses. Herrmann understood that and was trying to connect with an NFL team. He was supposed to have interviewed with Dallas in January, but nothing had come of it.

English, meanwhile, could not get a commitment for the defensive coordinator's job until Herrmann's fate was settled. So when Chicago came calling, he took the job.

This may have been one of the worst weeks in Carr's career. In his first 10 years at Michigan he had lost a total of three assistants to the pros. Michigan wasn't a place that one left lightly. Now two of them were going in the same week, and not of their own volition. He had to pull the plug on old friends, people who had been instrumental in securing his own professional and financial future. This is no small thing for someone like Carr.

On the other hand, losing English would loose the hounds. He wanted to ensure a soft landing for Herrmann, but not at this price. His entire legacy and the continuity of the Michigan football program was now being placed at risk.

Two days after announcing that he had taken the job with the Bears, English resigned it and returned to Ann Arbor with the title of sole defensive coordinator. And two days after that, the last shoe fell. Herrmann walked out of the Michigan locker room for the final time and accepted a job as linebackers coach with the New York Jets.

Carr flatly denied that he would have demoted Herrmann. "I knew Jim was going to have a job offer," he said. "I wanted to try and keep them both. But he'll do a great job in the NFL."

"My life is here," Herrmann told reporters on a day when a white winter blanket covered Ann Arbor. "I'll always be a Michigan man. Deep down, on a Saturday afternoon, I know where my heart is. But this is something I've always dreamt of, something I've always wanted to do. The pieces fell together at the right time."

They were brave words from a man who realized the only option left to him was to leave the place he had come to think of as his home for life and take one for the team.

Then he walked away. With that, the long season at The Big House was finally over.

A mere 162 days had passed since the kickoff of the Northern Illinois game. It seemed like a very long time ago. Aside from the events that landed Schembechler and Carr in the head coach's job, there rarely had been such a season of upheaval at Michigan.

But take a deep breath. Only 192 days from here to the kickoff with Vanderbilt.

Lloyd Carr Reflects

Q You have said that every season is a learning experience. What can you take away from a season like this last one?

A Every season presents its own challenges. Even when things are going well, when you have 120 people in the program—coaches, players—you are going to have some problems. You are going to have some issues, and some of those are not fun. You have to deal with injuries every year. And so I think this was as tough a challenge as I can remember for a team.

I was very disappointed; there is no question about that. But I am not disappointed in the people who played on this football team. I think they gave us everything they had, maintained great unity during some very difficult times, and I think they played their hearts out. But it just wasn't enough.

I think you can make a mistake when you gauge a team strictly by its record. This team could have folded. This team could have gone in the tank. When you lose like in the Wisconsin game on the last play of the game and you come back and go to Michigan State to play a team that's undefeated and ranked and an explosive team…

Here, when you lose, there are plenty of distractions, and that's part of the pressure that you have to deal with. And a lot of times, in any locker room…I don't care if it's junior high, high school, college, pros…when things go badly, there is always a tendency to point the finger. "Well, it wasn't my fault. You know, if Johnny over there had done a better job…"

This team didn't do that. They came back to work the next day. So I am extremely proud of the seniors. They were an unselfish group. They just kept fighting. Some people may not buy into that, but this team had a chemistry and they had good leadership. They played their final game of the regular season with a chance still to win the Big Ten, to even get into a BCS bowl. And with five minutes to go in the game, it was all there. So it's hard for me to be disappointed in a group of people who showed great grit and determination, toughness, passion, resilience. That to me is what the game will test. In those areas, this team met the challenge. Without it, they wouldn't have won some of those games.

I mean, when you think about the Penn State game—they have just taken the lead on us and they're kicking off and there's 52 seconds to go and you've got one timeout left. So in those circumstances people either quit and draw back, or they continue to believe and fight. This team did that.

Q You mentioned pressure. How much of that comes with the territory at Michigan, and how do you deal with it?

A I tell the kids I recruit that Michigan is not for everybody. I tell them it's hard here. You have to give a lot to succeed. You have to know how to embrace the pressure and make it a positive thing. Expectations are very high every year. Anything less than a Rose Bowl, at least, is considered a failure.

When you coach here, it doesn't take long to learn how high those standards are. It's hard. I've heard some coaches say they don't take the job home with them. But it consumes you. If you can't handle the criticism—if it tears you apart and if it distracts you—then you'll fail. You may fail anyway, but you have to be tough mentally because you know the pressure is real and it's intense. When you win, it's expected. When you lose…well, I hear the grumbling. Hey, every job has its drawbacks. The margin of error is very small. When you expend as much as we all do—emotionally and physically and mentally—and you fail, the best word, the most descriptive word, is *misery*.

It doesn't get more miserable for a coach or a player going to practice after losing. You are thinking about what happened last week and you know all the things that are out there and there are a lot of things trying to tear you apart in those circumstances. It takes some mental toughness to say, "Okay, we're not where we want to be, but let's go get ready this week. Let's go win again."

There was never a day when I got up in the morning last season that I wasn't looking forward to seeing these players. And every time I went into the meeting room to start the day, they were ready to go. You have to be able to go on. You can't be distracted by all the critics. I've seen people that in one way or another quit. It can be devastating and paralyzing. There is a part of you that wants to quit. It's the toughest part of the job, no question about it. It can get to a point where I'm sure it isn't worth it. But this university is 180 years old, and a football championship has to be measured against what that means.

Q **Were there ever moments during this season when self-pity entered into the equation?**

A I am not immune to it. Not in the inner sanctum of my own mind—a very small area. It doesn't do any good to talk about that. Sure, you can say a play here, a play there. But that's always true. You can lull yourself into not being realistic. To me it's all about the realistic evaluation of what we need to do to get better. It doesn't matter what day you are talking about; you are trying to get better. Now that the season is over you certainly have ample opportunity—although it's no more than the people you are competing against—to see if there are some things that you can do to get better and to go be what you want to be.

Q **So many of the games came down to making a late stop on defense. Is there a common theme to why it didn't seem to happen?**

A That was a big disappointment, although one of the things that an offense has got to do at the end of games is to be able to run the football to use the clock and protect your defense. But we just did not get that done. The thing that I can say unequivocally is that these guys played hard. They never quit. They fought their way back when a lot of teams wouldn't have. But we are deeply disappointed in the results, because even with all the things that we faced, we had chances and we weren't able to take them.

Q Did the problems on defense have to do with so many more teams using the spread offense?

A I think when you're dealing with spread teams that use three and four wide receivers, you have to take some risks. And we did. We blitzed Ohio State and hit their quarterback off the edge with a free blitzer a few times. But what he did in the last quarter of that game—I have got to give him credit. I mean Troy Smith is pretty good. We were not in a prevent defense on the last drive of that game. We were mixing our coverages. But with Smith you have to be right in his face, and he made absolutely incredible plays to evade tackles. If you don't get into the right gap on a blitz against him...

Yet when you are dealing with guys like Ted Ginn and Santonio Holmes, and they line them up in a lot of different situations, they create some problems for you. Offenses have the ability to move people around with motion to get into bunches. You don't get a lot of teams blitzing and playing man-to-man coverage without any secondary help. We played a significant amount of man coverage in that game. But you better take care of the quarterback first.

Q **Do you see a time when Michigan would use the spread?**

A I like what we do offensively. I think we will always be able to recruit great quarterbacks here, great tailbacks and wide receivers. I don't have any problem with the spread offense because I think it's had a lot of positive things. But to use a quarterback as a tailback is not something that I want to recruit to.

Q **Your offensive line was shredded with injuries. How significant a role did that play in your season?**

A The answer to that is very complex. We ran the football at times during this season extremely well, and at times we didn't. I am still trying to come to grips with that question. We felt we could run the football for 100 yards in any game. Had we been able to do that, I think the difference in this season would have been significant.

I think you have to take into consideration that Jake Long missed half the season and then played with an injury that had to be surgically repaired when the season ended. Adam Kraus didn't play at all at the end. Leo Henige broke his leg. Tim Massaquoi was out a good part of the year. Then Mike Hart went out. When all that happens, we're a different team. On the other hand, Mark Bihl had the opportunity to step in at center, and he earned my respect. He is quite a kid and improved significantly.

You still want to be able to run the football more effectively. But you have to adapt. But the answer is complex because we also played some outstanding defenses and players. A. J.

Hawk, for example. He makes some plays that only great players will make.

Q What progress can you point to this year?

A I think we made significant progress on defense. If you look at the statistics in the Big Ten, we did an excellent job. I think we're a much more physical team. I think our linebackers, particularly David Harris, will go into next season as guys [who are] going to have a chance to have really outstanding careers here. I think Prescott Burgess had a very good year. So there are a lot of guys that made big steps. We're not a great defense, but I think we have the nucleus of having the kind of defense we'd like next fall.

Q Chad Henne came in for a lot of criticism this year. There were some who say he took a step backward from his freshman year. How would you respond to that?

A The amazing thing is this kid is a sophomore. Chad Henne gave me confidence. It would be one thing if he was a senior quarterback. But he can influence me to make a decision that gives our team a chance to win in situations on the field that can go either way. You can make a lot of mistakes if you are greedy. But he can convince me.

Q How has the game changed since you began at Michigan?

A Everyone now has the ability to spread you out. It's not easy to stop them for four downs. But you still have to be able to run the football, and we weren't able to do that going back to the Wisconsin game. And defensively you still have to find a way to keep them out of the end zone. Regardless of what side of the ball you're on, those are the things that make the difference.

But many of the changes I've seen have to do with technology. It's a flat world in college football just like it is in everything else. That's made a huge difference in recruiting. Our coaches do a great job of getting on the right players early, and I think that's a critical issue with the recruiting services available today. You can communicate so much easier with high school coaches than you used to be able to. The exchange of videos is much quicker. There's nobody out there that isn't reachable constantly. There are a lot of things that make Michigan special—the tradition, the university, the educational opportunities. We've got a lot of things to sell when we recruit on the national level. But you can't be late on a lot of guys.

In today's football, you're also going to have a number of freshmen whose contributions can be the difference between winning and losing. The guy who caught the touchdown pass against Penn State was Mario Manningham, a freshman. But it's easy when a guy gets a lot of acclaim and has a very good year as a freshman and people write and pat him on the back to start believing all the hype. The guy that has the attitude, "Hey, I've got to get better, I've got to get stronger, I have to get better conditioned, I've got to learn more." Now you are dealing with a guy who has a chance to reach his potential. As a coach, that's why you can't spend a lot of time telling a guy how good he is. You have got to tell him how good he could be.

Q Speaking of technology, what about instant replay? It didn't work out for you in the Notre Dame and Nebraska games.

A If they're going to have instant replay, they have to have coaches' challenges. Because otherwise you have a guy in the booth that nobody knows, and he makes decisions on whether a play should be reviewed and we get no explanation. So then you use timeouts that you don't get back no matter what the final ruling is. We lost a timeout on a play in the Alamo Bowl where I saw clearly the ball was dropped, and that cost us. In terms of the rules going forward, the coaches' challenge has to be a part of it. Because it's only fair.

Q The vision of that 1997 championship is always present at Michigan. Is it, perhaps, too present?

A I've heard players say, "I'm tired of hearing about the '97 team." But the truth is they set the bar for all of us. They raised the expectations. I think the goal of every Michigan team since then is a national championship. I think we all recognize how difficult that is to do, but it is certainly a goal worth pursuing. I think we try to pursue that every season. And that's fun.

Appendix:
2005 Statistics

Game-by-Game Results

Michigan 33,
Northern Illinois 17

Rushing	Hart	117 yards
Receiving	Avant	127 yards
Passing	Henne	20-31, 227 yards
Tackles	Graham	10

1st	Henne to Avant	4 yards	9:34	7–0
1st	Henne to Hart	34 yards	0:20	14–3
2nd	Hart	2-yard run	8:48	20–10
2nd	Grady	1-yard run	0:27	27–10
4th	Rivas	FG 38 yards	13:16	30–10
4th	Rivas	FG 23 yards	9:14	33–10

Notre Dame 17, Michigan 10

Rushing	Grady	79 yards
Receiving	Avant	90 yards
Passing	Henne	19-44, 223 yards
Tackles	Mason	16

2nd Rivas	FG 38 yards	14:04	3–7
4th Henne to Manningham	25 yards	3:47	10–17

Michigan 55, Eastern Michigan 0

Rushing	Martin	128 yards
Receiving	Avant	93 yards
Passing	Henne	13-19, 147 yards
Tackles	Mason, Woodley	6

1st	Martin	1-yard run	13:03	7–0
1st	Martin	10-yard run	11:00	14–0
1st	Henne to Avant	14 yards	7:23	21–0
1st	Henne to Avant	26 yards	0:02	28–0
2nd	Henne to Thompson	6 yards	8:22	35–0
2nd	Rivas	FG 37 yards	0:24	38–0
3rd	Bloomsburgh	FG 21 yards	9:01	41–0
4th	Jackson	7-yard run	13:48	48–0
4th	Bradley	1-yard run	8:37	55–0

Michigan 20, Wisconsin 23

Rushing	Martin	91 yards
Receiving	Avant	108 yards
Passing	Henne	16-36, 258 yards
Tackles	Harris	7.5

2nd	Rivas	FG 44 yards	9:44	3–0
2nd	Henne to Avant	4 yards	4:27	10–0
2nd	Rivas	FG 28 yards	0:04	13–3
4th	Henne to Manningham	49 yards	9:03	20–16

Michigan 34,
Michigan State 31

Rushing	Hart	218 yards
Receiving	Avant	96 yards
Passing	Henne	26-35, 256 yards
Tackles	Englemon	13

1st Henne to Avant	3 yards	8:23	7–0
1st Henne to Manningham	43 yards	7:03	14–0
2nd Henne to Thompson	5 yards	11:20	21–7
2nd Rivas	FG 20 yards	0:09	24–21
4th Hart	1-yard run	11:29	31–24
OT Rivas	FG 35 yards		34–31

Michigan 20,
Minnesota 23

Rushing	Hart	109 yards
Receiving	Avant	73 yards
Passing	Henne	14-29, 155 yards
Tackles	Harris	18

1st Rivas	FG 23 yards	10:26	3–0
2nd Rivas	FG 47 yards	5:50	6–3
2nd Hart	1-yard run	3:10	13–3
3rd Breaston	95-yard kickoff return	12:25	20–13

Michigan 27,
Penn State 25

Rushing	Hart	108 yards
Receiving	Avant	75 yards
Passing	Henne	21-36, 212 yards
Tackles	Harris, Mason	10

2nd Rivas	FG 35 yards	4:34	3–0
3rd Hart	2-yard run	11:10	10–0
4th Henne to Manningham	2-point conversion, 33 yards	9:32	18–18
4th Rivas	FG 47 yards	3:45	21–18
4th Henne to Manningham	10 yards	0:00	27–25

Michigan 23, Iowa 20

Rushing	Grady	62 yards
Receiving	Avant	105 yards
Passing	Henne	14-21, 207 yards
Tackles	Mason	12

2nd Henne to Avant	5 yards	13:45	7–7
3rd Rivas	FG 26 yards	8:25	10–14
4th Henne to Breaston	52 yards	8:51	17–14
OT Jackson	1-yard run		23–20

Michigan 33, Northwestern 17

Rushing	Jackson	105 yards
Receiving	Avant	67 yards
Passing	Henne	17-30, 174 yards
Tackles	Burgess	7

1st	Grady	1-yard run	10:46	7–0
1st	Hall	83-yard fumble return	9:07	14–0
2nd	Rivas	FG 26 yards	9:09	17–10
2nd	Henne to Massey	10 yards	2:57	24–10
2nd	Rivas	FG 19 yards	0:58	27–10
4th	Rivas	FG 38 yards	13:29	30–17
4th	Rivas	FG 28 yards	7:11	33–17

Michigan 41, Indiana 14

Rushing	Grady	94 yards
Receiving	Avant	66 yards
Passing	Henne	17-24, 174 yards
Tackles	Harris	5

1st Henne to Ecker	5 yards	8:40	7–7
1st Henne to Avant	7 yards	5:49	14–7
2nd Grady	1-yard run	12:12	20–7
2nd Grady	32-yard run	5:58	27–7
2nd Jackson	6-yard run	2:45	34–7
2nd Henne to Breaston	11 yards	0:23	41–7

Michigan 21, Ohio State 23

Rushing	Hart	15 yards
Receiving	Manningham	64 yards
Passing	Henne	25-36, 223 yards
Tackles	Burgess	10

2nd Henne to Avant	2 yards	5:18	7–9
3rd Rivas	FG 27 yards	10:01	10–12
3rd Grady	2-point conversion, 2 yards	1:20	18–12
4th Rivas	FG 19 yards	7:49	21–12

Michigan 28,
Nebraska 32

Rushing	Hart	74 yards
Receiving	Avant	71 yards
Passing	Henne	21-43, 270 yards
Tackles	Barringer	9

1st Henne to Ecker	13 yards	5:48	7–7
2nd Henne to Massey	16 yards	11:43	14–7
3rd Henne to Manningham	21 yards	6:31	21–17
4th Henne	1-yard run	11:40	28–17

Season Leaders

Rushing

Hart	662 yards
Grady	483 yards
Jackson	228 yards
Martin	226 yards
Breaston	101 yards

Receiving

Avant	1,007 yards
Manningham	433 yards
Breaston	291 yards
Ecker	285 yards
Hart	154 yards

Passing

Henne	223-382	2,526 yards

Scoring

Rivas	90 points
Avant	48 points
Manningham	36 points
Hart	32 points
Grady	30 points

Team Scoring

Michigan 345, Opponents 244

Tackles

Harris	88
Mason	85
Burgess	81
Hall	61
Woodley	48